How To Really Play The Piano

...the stuff your teacher never taught you.

Bill Hilton

Carrier Books

CARRIER BOOKS

2 Tanrallt, Rachub, Bangor, Gwynedd, LL57 3HB

www.carrierbooks.com

First published in Great Britain in 2009

Copyright © Bill Hilton 2009

Bill Hilton has asserted his right under the Copyright, Designs and Patents Act 1988 to be identified as the author of this work.

A CIP catalogue record for this book is available from the British Library.

ISBN 0956220401

Printed by Lightning Source UK Ltd, Milton Keynes.

For Graeme Allen, Sarah Beecroft, Matt Nixon and Mike Selby

What you need to know to use this book

How To Really Play The Piano is not for absolute beginners. To get the most out of what follows, you should be able to:

- **Play easy pieces with both hands together** – or, if you've been away from the piano for a few years, have the basic skills and willingness to get back to this level.

- **Read music in both treble and bass clef.** You don't need to be a fluent or fast reader of music – still less a sight-reader – but you need an idea of which notes are where on the page and on the piano, and to be able to read and interpret standard rhythms, including dotted rhythms.

- **Make sense of elementary music theory**. The most important things to understand are key signatures and the scales associated with major and minor keys. You also need to know a little about intervals, a topic that isn't always covered in basic piano lessons. As such, I've included a short overview of intervals in Appendix 1, where you'll also find a list of resources that will help you if you need reminding of any other aspects of theory.

If you've reached Grade 3 or 4 standard (Associated Board or similar) you'll be fine. Even if you've only done Grade 1 or Grade 2 you should get by pretty well. Don't worry if some of the examples in the book look difficult: most are included for analysis rather than performance.

If your lessons were a long time ago and you feel you need a refresher, you may find it's just a case of sitting down at the keyboard and re-familiarising yourself with the instrument. If you need some more serious reminding, a teach-yourself guide may come in useful. The best available is probably Kenneth Baker's classic, *The Complete Piano Player*. Better still, talk to a piano teacher about a few refresher lessons. If you've had lessons in the past, it shouldn't take long to get up to speed.

Contents

Acknowledgements

This book is the result of a lot of discussion over the years, and it's going to be difficult to name everyone who has made some sort of contribution. Still, here goes.

Thanks, first, to everyone who has taught me piano, formally or informally: Jacqui Umpleby, David Wright, Richard Seymour, Peter Harding, Harvey Davies and Jana Frenklova. Nick Fitton and Lee Hextall encouraged my early jazz and blues playing. Without Jacqui and Nick, in particular, this book wouldn't exist.

When I had the idea for the book, Alex Needham was the first person I told. Alex is a great pianist himself, and was both encouraging and enthusiastic. He may not recall the event, as we were enjoying rather a large night out at the time, but he has my gratitude all the same.

I co-wrote my last book with Mike Pywell, who gave some valuable early insights into the style and approach of this one, as well as how it might be marketed. I would also like to mention John Elliott, who wrote his book *Insights in Jazz* at the same time I was writing this, and with whom I spent a useful hour on the phone discussing ideas. I haven't had time to read *Insights* at the time of writing, but other people seem to like it a lot, and on that basis I would recommend it: more info at www.dropback.co.uk.

Matt Bourne generously gave his time to help with file conversion. Paul and Emma Telfer helped a lot - though they may not have realised it at the time - by sharing their experiences of small-scale publishing.

Sarah Beecroft, who was originally going to be a co-author, and subsequently became a dedicatee when the demands of her career caught up with her, offered some brilliant insights during the planning stages.

Andrew James gave me some useful tips on getting the best scoring results out of Finale, while Dave Beck advised on readability and design. Between them, Jen Pearson, James Mavin and Christina Les read, checked and commented on the whole book.

Any errors that remain are, needless to say, entirely my responsibility.

Rachub, October 2009.

Introduction

If you've ever had piano lessons, you'll know most piano education is based on playing lots of classical music and lots of scales. There's nothing wrong with that, especially if it's your ambition to become a competent classical musician.

But the chances are your piano teacher never taught you a lot of the stuff you really wanted to learn. I was lucky: as well as having an outstanding classical teacher, I learned to improvise, play jazz and blues, pick up pop songs, play from chord charts, accompany singers and play in bands. I learned to play like Jools Holland, Elton John, Ben Folds and Jamie Cullum (though I wouldn't claim to be as good as them). My friends, many of whom played the piano themselves, used to ask me how I did it. This book is an attempt to answer that question.

How to get started

Over the following pages you'll find lots of examples and quite a few suggested learning techniques, but very few must-play exercises. Neither does the book have a rigid structure: if you're uncertain about the basics, you're probably best off taking the sections in order. But if you're a more confident player, you'll get the most benefit if you skip around and focus on the material that interests you, dipping in and out as necessary. To get you started, here are five suggestions:

1. Read the technical sections when you're actually seated at your piano or keyboard. That way, you'll be able to park your fingers on the notes and start playing around with ideas as soon as you come across them.

2. When you're improvising, remember there's no such thing as a 'wrong' note. Some notes sound better than others at some times, but that's all. Whatever you do, don't get hung up on making everything sound 'right'.

3. You should play to please yourself more than anyone else. If it sounds good to you and you enjoy it, that's the most important thing.

4. You might find it useful to have one or two songbooks handy: perhaps a couple of compilations of film songs, Broadway show tunes or pop classics. Anything that has a piano-vocal score (see p.70) and chord markings will do the job, helping you to try out many principles and ideas – especially the ones in Parts 1 and 3 – as you go along.

5. Once you start playing around with musical ideas, *really* play around. Experiment, mess about, play chords and riffs and other bits and pieces over and over again. As we will see in Part 4, effective practice is all about exploration, testing your limits and enjoying yourself.

An open-minded approach is essential. Learning specific techniques will take you a long way, but the secret of success lies in your willingness to spend long periods of time sitting at the piano, getting frustrated, making discoveries and pushing the boundaries of what you can do.

A note on terms
Throughout the book I use *pop piano* as shorthand for the collection of skills we're dealing with, using 'pop' in a broad sense. 'Popular music' means 'the music of the people', and includes what we conventionally describe as pop music along with rock, jazz, folk, country, bluegrass, newgrass, roots music, Motown, soul, the blues and much more. The skills we're going to look at are common to nearly all popular music.

Another shorthand is the word *song*. Most popular music takes the form of song, but not all. However, terms like 'piece' and 'piece of music' are a bit clumsy. 'Song' is nice and clear, and when I use it you should take it to refer to any piece of popular music, whether that piece has words or not.

Watching and listening

When you're working on skills like improvisation you'll get a lot of benefit from listening to and watching other pianists. In fact, watching can be more useful than listening. It's difficult to pick up specific techniques by ear, even if you're a good player.

If you have web access there are hundreds of useful videos on YouTube.com. Search for terms like 'piano improvisation', 'jazz piano', and 'rock piano', and you'll find hours of material to watch, entirely free. If you turn to Appendix 3 you'll also find a list of DVDs of famous pianists in action. At various points I'll suggest specific videos to watch, including video tutorials I've created to tie in with the material in the book. I appreciate not everybody has fast web access, but take a look if you can. You'll find a list of the tie-in tutorials at:

www.jamcast.co.uk/book

And finally...

Nothing worthwhile is easy, and mastering what follows will take time and effort. You'll make mistakes, you'll find some bits difficult, and every now and then you'll probably get frustrated because your fingers won't do what your brain is telling them to. Don't worry: that's just a sign that you're doing it right. Making mistakes is an essential part of the learning process. The single best piece of advice I can give you is 'stick at it'. If you do, you *will* see results.

I started learning these skills in my school jazz band, when I was twelve. I'd been having classical piano lessons for a few years, but learning improvisation and comping was hard. Other band members helped me, scribbling down chords and left hand ideas during lunchtime rehearsals.

Most of it I just worked out for myself. I'd have made much quicker progress if I'd had a book that gave me the knowledge I needed to take my beginner's ability at classical piano and turn it in the direction of jazz, blues and pop. Not a book that held my hand and set out a formula for piano success – that would be impossible – but one that gave me a foundation of knowledge, some suggestions about how I might apply it, and the freedom to learn in my own way. That's the book I've tried to write.

1. Understanding Harmony

If you want to achieve anything on the piano beyond playing from sheet music, it's essential you understand basic harmony.

That means getting your head around chords and chord progressions. Knowing a bit of elementary music theory is going to help with this: you can refresh your memory of terms and concepts – including intervals, which are important here – by using the resources in Appendix 1.

Harmony is the closest pop piano gets to rocket science, but it isn't difficult if you approach it the right way. Three pieces of advice on how to use the material in this part of the book:

1. The very best way of grasping what follows is to play the examples, which aren't particularly hard. Some of the concepts may seem complex, but they will become much clearer when you hear them at work. I've created several video tutorials that should also help to make things clearer. You can find them indexed under 'Understanding Harmony' at:

www.jamcast.co.uk/book

2. You don't need to learn all this stuff off by heart before moving on. Here's a good strategy: skim through for now, getting a feel for the basic terms and ideas and playing through the examples. Then, when you're working through later sections of the book, refer back to this section to reinforce your understanding. If you try to make sense of it all first time around, it will seem like very heavy going!

3. Experimentation is cool. Feel free to mess around with the material in this section. The best way to understand harmony is to explore it and discover for yourself what the different sounds can do.

What are chords?

Take a look at the version of *We Wish You A Merry Christmas* below. As you'll see, all your hands are doing is playing simple blocks of notes – there's no melody in the piano part. I've included the melody and the lyrics in a separate stave over the top, so you can sing or hum along as you play.

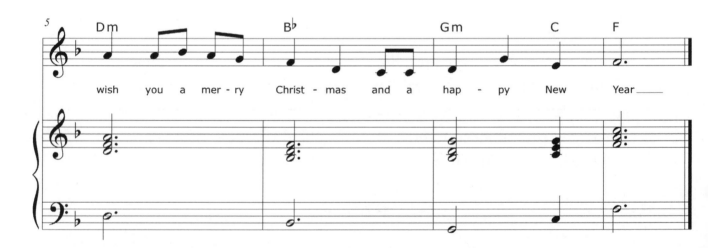

Those blocks of notes you're playing are chords. The symbols above each block, on the melody line, don't refer to the names of notes. They are the names of the chords: F, Dm and so on. Play through the piano part again, singing, humming or imagining the melody line as you go. When you've done that, take a look at the version on the next page - it's still the same song, but with some slight changes:

In this second version the chords are made up of different patterns of notes, but they still work with the melody. They are still the same chords, just played differently. There are hundreds of different ways of playing each basic chord. If you're coming from an instrument like the guitar, on which each chord can be played in just a handful of ways, the huge number of variations available to pianists might take some getting used to.

The first chord in both our versions of *We Wish You A Merry Christmas* is F - as we would expect it to be in most (but not all) songs in the key of F major. Here are six different ways of playing the chord of F on the piano, using two hands:

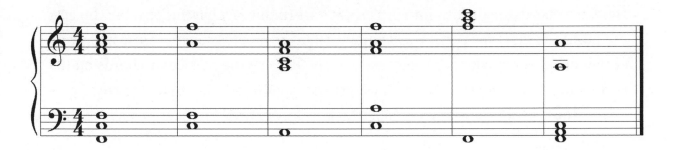

Similarly, the third chord is Gm ('G minor'). Here are some ways of playing it:

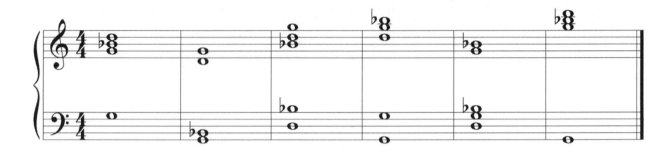

Although all those chords look very different from one another, what they have in common are the notes that make them up. Every single one of the F chords on the previous page is made up of some combination of the notes F, A and C. Likewise, each of the Gm chords above is made up of some combination of the notes G, B♭ and D.

That's all a chord is: a combination of notes played together to produce a particular sound. Some chords sound harmonious, some sound jangly and awkward ('discordant'). If you've learned some basic music theory as part of your piano lessons, you might be under the impression that 'proper' chords are the ones that sound neat, nice or 'right'. That's not true: a jazz pianist, for example, will tell you that any combination of notes can be considered a chord. There are thousands of possible chords you can play on a piano keyboard by using different notes in the left and right hands and varying your *voicings* and *inversions* (you'll find those terms explained on pp20-21). As we'll see, some chords are much more common than others.

Chords are organised into sequences (often referred to as *progressions*) that underlie a song's melody. You'll sometimes also hear musicians talking about *the chord changes* (or just *the changes*) when they are referring to a song's chord progression. Let's go back to the chord symbols above the melody line in *We Wish You A Merry Christmas*. Here they are again, written as a basic progression:[1]

F | B♭ | Gm | C | Dm | B♭ | Gm, C | F |

Here, the chords are divided into three-beat bars (in the last bar but one, the Gm gets two beats and the C one beat). You'll notice that in the progression there's no indication of the melody or rhythm, or even how you should play the particular chords on the keyboard. It's just the bare-bones harmony that goes under the tune. You could play each of those chords however you liked. So long as you used the right notes in each

---

1. This isn't the only possible progression for *We Wish You*. It's a traditional melody that works with several different harmonic options. I've chosen one that best reflects the basic chords of the key, a concept we'll discuss on p17.

chord, and played the chords in that order, you'd *always* be able to sing *We Wish You A Merry Christmas* over the top.

What's important here isn't the individual chords, or the key, but the pattern of the progression. We could move the chord progression into another major key (to use the technical term, we'd *transpose* it) and, as long as the relationships between the chords remained the same, we could still hum or sing the tune above them.

Below is a version of *We Wish You A Merry Christmas* in A major rather than F major. Compared to the version in F, every note and chord has been moved up an interval of a major third, which is four semitones.[2] All the chords are different, but it's still very much the same song:

2. A major third is a type of *interval* - you'll find an explanation of what intervals are and how they work in Appendix 1, with a link to a video tutorial. A *semitone* is one of the the units in which intervals are measured. It's the distance between any note on the keyboard and the note to its *immediate* right or left, whether that note is white or black. So, for example, the note a semitone above G is G# (A♭) and the note a semitone below G is F# (G♭). Two semitones make a *whole tone*. The note a whole tone above C is D, and the note a whole tone below C is B♭ (A#).

So we can either say that A is four semitones above F (F# is one semitone above; G two semitones; G# three semitones; A four semitones) or that A is two whole tones above F.

15

You'll notice that as the key and the notes have changed, so have the chord symbols above the melody line. Here they are stripped out:

A | D | Bm | E | F#m | D | Bm, E | A |

There are a couple of ways in which you might already have come across chords. First, if you took piano lessons to a moderate level you'll have learned about *triads* and their *inversions*. A triad is a type of three-note chord. The most common ones - major and minor triads - are made up of a *root* note (the note the chord gets its name from) plus the note an interval of a major or minor third above the root, plus the note an interval of a perfect fifth above the root.[3]

Below are two examples of the chord of C major in the form of triads. The first starts on middle C, the second on the C above middle C:

As you can see, the triad is made up of the notes of C (the root note), E (a major third above C) and G (a perfect fifth above C).

Both triads are in what we call *root position*, because the root is the lowest note in the chord. You don't have to play a C chord as a triad – it could be made up of lots more notes, as long as they were all Cs, Es or Gs. Triads are important, though, and I'll discuss them some more below.

Basic chords and chord notation

Depending how far you got with your piano lessons, you might also have looked at formal chord notation, which uses capital Roman numerals (I, II, III, IV, V, VI, VII) to describe chords independent of key. Each key, major and minor, contains a number of basic chords – they are the ones that tend to pop up most often in pieces of music written in that key.

In the key of C major the main, or *tonic*, chord (C major itself, as written above) is chord I, because it's based on the first note of the scale of C major; the chord based on the second note of the scale, Dm ('D minor'), is II; Em, which is based on the third note of the scale, is III, and so on.

3. A perfect fifth is another type of interval. Again, if you're not sure about intervals, have a look at Appendix 1 and/or the video on intervals listed at www.jamcast.co.uk/book.

If that sounds complicated, here it is written out – first, we take the scale of C major:

Then we create the basic chords in the key of C major by building a triad on each note of the scale, using only notes from that key – some will be minor chords, some major:

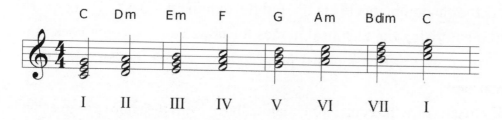

It works the same way in every major key. You create the basic chords – there are seven of them - by building a root position triad on each note of the scale. Notice that the first chord and the final chord are both labelled 'I' – that's because, although they are an octave apart, they are the same chord: C.

That gives us C, Dm, Em, F, G, Am and Bdim[4] as the main chords in the key of C major. Of course, they aren't the only chords you might come across in a piece of music in C: composers and songwriters often add harmonic depth by elaborating on the basic chords (using chords like Am7 instead of Am, for example), or by using chords from 'outside' the key. But if you have a piece of music in C major, most of the chords, more often than not, will be based on that list.

It's also worth knowing that the different chords have technical names. The most important ones are:

- *Tonic* for the I chord – C in the key of C major
- *Subdominant* for the IV chord – F in the key of C major
- *Dominant* for the V chord – G in the key of C major.

By way of comparison, here is the scale of F major:

---

4. The Bdim above the seventh note of the scale indicates a diminished chord - more on these below.

...and the main chords built on it:

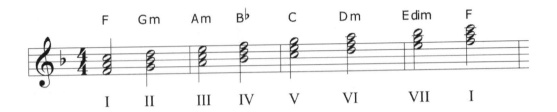

The tonic (I) is F; the subdominant (IV) is B♭ and the dominant (V) is C. Don't worry too much about memorising the technical names for now. You can come back and revisit them as we go on to discuss chord progressions, where the concepts they describe are important.

(By the way, if you compare the chords of F major, above, with the chord progression that featured in our first two versions of *We Wish You A Merry Christmas*, which are in F, you'll see that every chord in the song is one of the basic chords of the key.)

Chords in minor keys

Minor key harmony is a bit peculiar. Here is an F minor scale:

And the chords that are, in theory, built on that scale:

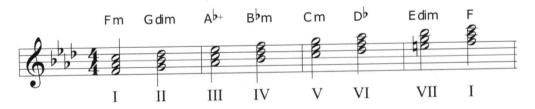

The complexity arises because there's more than one type of minor scale. If you got sufficiently far with piano lessons, you'll have played both *harmonic* and *melodic* minor scales, which are different from one another, and the basis for different sets of chords. The F minor example above is a harmonic minor scale. To complicate things further, the chords based on it aren't the ones that crop up most often in minor-key popular songs. Songs in F minor would most commonly use Fm, Gm, A♭, B♭m, C and D♭ and their variations (Gm7, .B♭m6, C, and so on - see below for definitions.)

This is all pretty academic, and you'll rarely need to know about it in day-to-day piano playing. It's just useful to know that these complexities exist.

Using Roman notation

Remember our chord sequence for *We Wish You A Merry Christmas*? Written out with letter symbols, it looks like this in F major:

F | B♭ | Gm | C | Dm | B♭ | Gm, C | F |

If you refer to the chart of chords in the key of F major at the top of the previous page, you'll see we don't have to use the letter chord symbols – we can use numerals instead:

I | IV | IIm | V | VIm | IV | IIm, V | I |

...which is really useful for talking about chord progressions in a way that isn't tied to a particular key. You won't actually come across Roman notation much when you play, but it's useful to know how it works when you do meet it. In conversation, and sometimes in writing, those numerals are pronounced 'first', 'fourth' and 'fifth', or sometimes 'one', 'four', 'five'.

The system of using the letter names of specific chords (F, Dm and so on) is what musicians are usually talking about when they refer to 'chord notation'. The individual symbols are known, simply, as 'chord symbols'. Classical piano teaching mostly ignores this kind of chord notation, but, in tandem with the five-line stave, it's the most useful method of notating popular music.

In the rest of this section we'll focus on lettered chord notation in our discussion of harmony, except in those instances where it's useful to talk about chords in an abstract way, when we'll use the I, IV, V Roman notation system.

Types of chord

Speaking very broadly, there are two main types of chord: straightforward major and minor chords, which, whatever their size and spread on the keyboard, are made up of combinations of just three basic notes; and more complex chords with four or more basic notes in them. (A combination of just two notes is probably better referred to as a harmonic interval - see p106 in Appendix 1 for details.)

Triads

We've already met the triad – a common chord of three notes, all within a single octave (or, to put it in a way that's more theoretically correct for major and minor triads, a three-note chord in which the notes are separated by thirds when played in root position). Just to be clear, these chords are all (major) triads:

While these chords aren't:

It might be worth playing through both sets of examples a couple of times to get your ear and your fingers used to the difference between triads and other chords.

The 'I' chord of any given key (see pp16-17) is made up of the first, third and fifth notes of the scale of that key, and is known as the *tonic triad*. So the tonic triad of C major is made up of C (the first note of the scale, or 'tonic'), E (the third note of the scale) and G (the fifth note of the scale).

Triad inversions

You'll notice that not all of the triads in the example above are played in root position (i.e., with the root of the chord as its lowest note – see p16). The triads that aren't in root position are *inversions*.

Below is the chord of C in its root position, then its *first inversion* (with E as the lowest note of the chord), then its *second inversion* (with G as the lowest note). Again, you could play these shapes in any octave and they would still be C chords:

root position   1st inversion   2nd inversion

As well as *inversion*, another term you'll hear that relates to the way chords are played is *voicing* – the F and Gm examples on pp13-14, above, are different voicings of those particular chords. The terms overlap, but these are the rough differences:

• **Inversion** refers to the order you play a chord's notes in, from bottom to top.
• **Voicing** refers to the combination of notes you use in a particular chord.

So, if you play the notes E, G and C in that pitch order in the same octave, that's an inversion – the first inversion of the C major triad, which we looked at above. On the other hand, If you play a C and a G in your left hand and an E and a C an octave higher in your right, that's a particular voicing of the chord of C. There are many more voicings than inversions.

As we saw in the example of *We Wish You A Merry Christmas* chords remain the same in terms of their harmonic effect, no matter which voicing or inversion they are played in. You can still hum or sing the same tune over the top of different voicings and inversions of the same chord progression.

The dominant seventh
The basic major and minor triads form the harmonic foundation of all western music. All other chords can be viewed as enhancements or adaptations of the basic triads. We'll cover all the most important ones when we look at the structure of individual chords. For now, however, let's take a closer look at just one of the complex chords: the dominant seventh.

This is a major chord with a minor (flattened) seventh added, and, as we'll see on p24, it plays an important role in harmony. Below is a C major, dominant seventh chord, which would be notated as C7 (usually pronounced 'C seven'):

You create the dominant seventh by playing a triad in its root position and then adding the note that lies a minor third (three semitones) above the fifth, the highest note in the triad. So the highest note in the triad of C major, played in the root position, is G:

...and the note three semitones above that is B♭, which is added to make the C7 chord:

You can invert it, too: C7 has a root position and (because it contains four possible starting notes, rather than a triad's three) three basic inversions:

Try forming a few dominant sevenths of your own. Select some major triads – say, A, F, G♭ and B – and work out what A7, F7, G♭7 and B7 would be. If you're not sure of the notes in those triads, check the tables in Appendix 2. When forming the chords, listen for the distinctive dominant seventh sound that you encountered with C7.

Resolution[5]

At its simplest, *resolution* is about how certain types of chord lead naturally to others. Mostly commonly, it's used to describe how some chords create an expectation of returning (or *resolving*) to the tonic chord of the key at the end of a phrase, section or entire song. Remember, the tonic chord is the main chord of any key – E♭ for the key of E♭ major, Am for the key of A minor. It's worth bearing in mind that the tonic chord on which a progression finishes won't necessarily be a simple chord. For example, a progression in C might end on a C6 or Cmaj7 chord. More on those later.

5. I've created a video tutorial on resolution. You can find it here:

www.jamcast.co.uk/piano-chord-progressions-dominant-chords/

The chord that most obviously resolves on to the tonic is called the *dominant*. If you play a C chord, then a G chord, then return to the C, you should notice quite a strong resolving effect:

You don't get the same effect if you play – for example – a C followed by an Am before returning to the C:

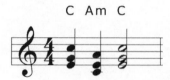

The Am chord just doesn't want to go back to the C as much as the G does. That's because in C major, G is the dominant chord. The dominant, which is the chord based on the fifth note of the scale, whatever key you're in, always offers a natural resolution back to the tonic chord.

So the dominant of C major is G major; of G major, D major; of A minor, E major. That's right: minor tonic chords still have major dominants. Here are some examples, in both major and minor keys. First, the key of A minor, where E is the dominant:

A major, where, as in A minor, E is also the dominant:

E♭ major, where B♭ is the dominant:

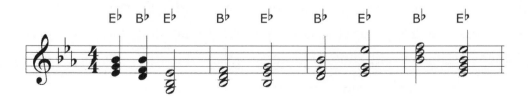

And C minor, where the dominant is G:

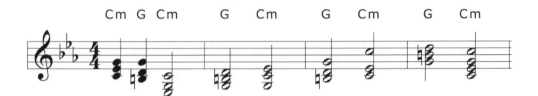

Dominant chords often have minor sevenths added to them to make dominant seventh chords, which we examined above. If you play D dominant seventh (D7), you can hear that it really, really wants to resolve on to G (or Gm) – more so than the standard dominant, D. If you play through this sequence you'll notice that the D7→G resolutions are stronger than the D→G resolutions:

Likewise, E7 wants to resolve on to an A or an Am chord. It's much stronger than a straightforward E chord, the plain dominant in the keys of A major and A minor. Here's a comparison of the two at work in A minor:

The thing is, the dominant isn't the only chord you can use to resolve to the tonic, and from a composer's or improviser's point of view it's not always the best choice, either. A dominant→tonic resolution, especially if the dominant has an added seventh, such as D7→G, can actually sound a bit cheesy and 'pat'.

If you're in the key of G major, below is a list of some of the chords that will resolve on to the tonic, with greater or lesser degrees of strength:

$$D, D7, C, C/D, Cmaj7/D, Am/D \rightarrow \mathbf{G}$$

(N.B. 'C/D' means 'a chord of C with a D in the bass' – we'll find out more about these bass voicings below). Here are those chords written out. Remember that this is just one example of the possible voicings and inversions you could use:

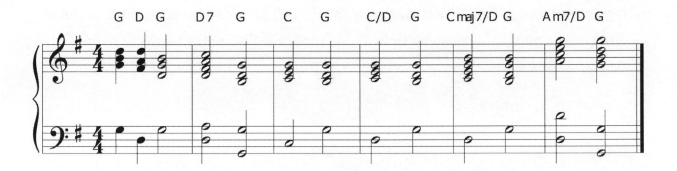

Those are chords based on the fifth (D), fourth (C) and second (A) notes of the scale. In the key of E major, they would look like this:

B, B7, A, A/B, Amaj7/B, F#m/B → **E**

And an example of how they could be played:

In a minor key, your choices are a bit more limited, but not by much. In the key of A minor you can resolve to the tonic chord using...

E   E7   Dm7 (bit weak) F (weaker still) → **Am**

A written example of those chords:

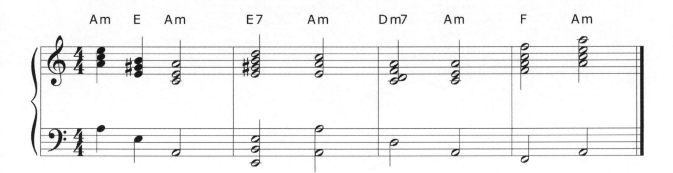

25

Different dominant and dominant-type chords will give your resolutions a slightly different flavour. Whereas a straight G or G7→G resolution sounds very clean and straightforward...

...Cmaj7/D→G sounds much more rich and lush:

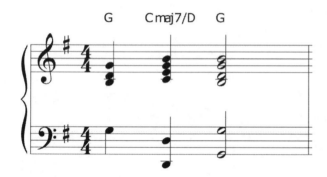

You can make the Cmaj7/D even lusher by dropping the E to an E♭ for a major/minor sound, or by adding a D - (i.e., a ninth; see p34.)

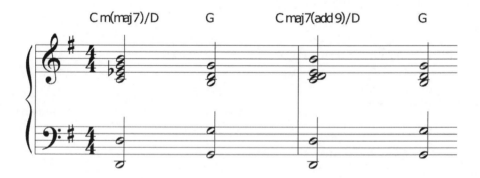

Finally, bear in mind that the dominant doesn't have to resolve on to the tonic - it can go more or less anywhere: in G major, it could go D7→Am, D7→C and so on:

How chord progressions work[6]

Now let's deal with a really important concept that goes to the heart of western music and 99.99% of everything you'll ever play on the piano. Sequences of chords are called *progressions* because that's exactly what they do – progress. With the exception of some types of electronica and experimentalism, every piece of western music, whether it's a song or a symphony, is a journey from one point to another, usually via a number of different stops along the way.

From the point of view of harmony, the important point to remember is that the 'journey' of any particular piece of music begins and ends at the tonic chord. It may stray a long way from that chord, but eventually, via the process of resolution described above, it will come back home. When we listen to a chord sequence like this...

$$E\flat \mid Fm \mid Gm \mid A\flat \mid B\flat7 \mid Eb$$

...we're hearing a full journey, from tonic, out, and back again. Here's one way that sequence could work as the harmony for a piece of simple piano music:

/Cont...

6.Related video tutorial:

www.jamcast.co.uk/how-chord-progressions-work/

Of course, the 'home' point – the tonic chord – can change. That's a process called modulation, though it's often just referred to as 'key change'. It's very common in classical music and in certain types of popular songs (especially show and film music – listen to a contemporary Disney song from a film like *The Lion King* and you might hear anything up to four or five semitone modulations). Below is an example of a semi-tone key change of a sort you might hear in popular songs. It's moving from the key of C major to the key of D♭ major:

C | Am7 | F | G | A♭ | D♭ [...]

Here's an example of a piece of music with that chord sequence:

Playing through that progression a few times will help you understand how powerful the dominant chord is when it comes to setting the key of a piece of music. The sequence is in C major, but A♭7 is a strong dominant in D♭ major, so as soon as the A♭7 arrives the progression stops 'wanting' to resolve to C and starts 'wanting' to resolve to D♭. It doesn't have to, but that's where the flow of the music seems to go.

Structures of individual chords

There follows a short guide to the most common chords you'll come across when you're playing from piano-vocal scores or lead sheets. This is by no means an exhaustive list – it's just intended to help you understand how the majority of chord symbols work.

Don't forget that there are look-up tables of the important chords in all the major and minor keys in Appendix 2. Additionally, semitones and tones are important here: if you need reminding of how they work, check the note on p15.

IF IN DOUBT, DON'T READ – PLAY.

It's MUCH more important to get a sense of the sounds of the chords, the shapes under your fingers and their names than it is to understand the theory behind them.

While it's worth skimming these chord descriptions now and playing through the examples, there's no need to start learning them off by heart. Instead, get stuck into Parts 3 and 4, getting used to the chord sounds and shapes through practice. Revisit this section as and when you come across a chord you're a bit hazy about.

Note: by convention, major chords are simply referred to by their letters: so 'A♭' refers to A♭ major. Minor chords are always specified as such. As well as being spelled out in notation (C = C major; Cm = C minor), you can hear this in conversation between musicians, who will refer to a chord of E♭ major simply as 'E flat', but will always refer to the minor chord based on the same root as 'E flat minor'.

The same is true, to an extent, of keys. If someone says 'let's play this in C' they always mean C major. If they meant C minor, they would say 'C minor'.

Major

Symbol: just the letter of the chord: C, E, F#, B♭ and so on.

A basic chord which, when played as a triad in its first inversion, includes a root, a major third (four semitones above the root) and a perfect fifth (three semitones above the major third). A common voicing is constructed by adding a second root note, an octave above the first. These are all major chords:

The chord of F major (usually just referred to as 'F' – see note on previous page) has F as its root note; the major third is A, and the perfect fifth is C:

The chord of C# major (identical to D♭ major) has C# as its root; E# (F) as its major third, and G# as its perfect fifth:

Major Seventh

Symbol: maj7 (Gmaj7, A♭maj7). You sometimes also see it as M7, with a capital 'M', whereas minor sevenths always have a lower-case 'm'. However, many writers tend to avoid this style, as it can cause confusion.

The major seventh chord pretty much does what it says on the tin: it's a major chord with an added major seventh. The major seventh is the note eleven semitones up (or, more simply, a semitone down) from the root note of the chord.

For example, the major seventh note in the C major scale is B, giving a chord that looks like this (remember you're playing a B natural, not a B♭!):

In the key of E major the seventh note is D#, giving a chord that looks like this:

So to create a major seventh chord, you simply stick your major seventh note anywhere in a major chord. Because a major seventh chord contains four different notes (unlike a straightforward major or minor chord, which only has three) it has a root position and *three* possible inversions, rather than two – as you can see in the examples above.

If you play the example chords you'll notice that major sevenths have quite a rich, dreamy sound. They are very common in popular music from the 1930s to the 1960s and became a staple jazz chord after the genre began to move away from its roots in the blues, ragtime and marching band music in the years leading up to the Second World War. You can still hear them in the work of modern songwriters, although it's now more common to hear a major seventh as a passing chord or a chord in a development section rather than as the first or last chord of a progression.

You can add a major seventh to a minor chord (a 'minor major seventh'):

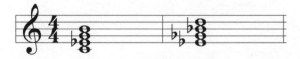

That's quite a common chord in jazz, but one that is difficult to notate. I usually write something like Cm(maj7), Cm + maj7, Cm/maj7 or CmM7 – a bit sloppy in terms of music theory, but good enough for practical purposes.

Sixth (Major and Minor)
Symbol: 6 (E♭6, B6, G6) for major chords, m6 (Cm6, B♭m6, Am6) for minor chords.

Another important jazz chord, the **major sixth** is often used in similar ways to the major seventh, except it uses the note a major sixth (nine semitones above the tonic) rather than the major seventh. So, to form C6 you would add an A to the basic chord of C; E♭6 is an E♭ chord with an added C; D6 is a D chord with an added B, and so on:

As a point of interest (one that you don't really need to commit to memory now, so don't panic if this sounds a bit technical...) any given major sixth is identical to a separate minor seventh chord[7] – the one rooted on the added sixth note. So, to take an example, C6 contains the notes C-E-G-A, as does Am7. Which symbol you use to describe the chord usually depends on context, and doesn't really matter very much from the point of view of general musicianship or playing for fun.

The **minor sixth** is only slightly different. It's identical to its major equivalent in every way except it contains a minor third rather than a major third. So, to form Cm6 you would add an A to a Cm chord in the same way you'd add an A to a C chord to form C6. If you've learnt some music theory this might confuse you a bit, because in most forms of the minor scale the sixth is a semitone lower than in the major scale, giving A♭ as the 'sixth' for Cm. Without digging deep into the difference between harmonic and melodic minor scales, suffice to say you actually use the same 'sixth' note as you would for the major sixth chord. Confused? Play the examples below and listen to it all make sense before your very ears:

Dominant Seventh ('seventh')
Symbol: 7 (C7, G7, F7)

The dominant seventh is a very different beast from the major seventh, both in terms of the way it's used and the way it sounds - though superficially the difference between the two chords is slight. As we saw above, dominant seventh chords are often just referred to as 'sevenths' or – in conversation – as 'C seven', 'F seven' and so on.

---

7. Minor sevenths are covered on p40.

You form the dominant seventh by adding a *minor* seventh (the note 10 semitones above, or two semitones below, the root note) to a *major* chord. So, to form C7 you add a B♭ to a C major triad; to form A7 you add a G (natural) to an A major triad:

The effect a dominant seventh has depends on its context in a piece of music. As we've seen in the section on resolution, if the major chord based on the fifth note of the key of a piece of music (the dominant) is made into a seventh, it enhances the resolving effect of the chord. If any other major chords in the key are made into sevenths it creates a strong 'bluesy' effect. Play through the following sequence in C major:

C | G7 | C | F7 | C |

Here's a notated example:

You'll notice that the G7 (the chord based on the fifth note of the scale of the key, C major) sounds very natural and resolves strongly on to the C. That's why they're called 'dominant sevenths' – because working as a dominant chord is their most obvious role. But dominant sevenths don't need to be in the dominant position in a key: if you listen to the F7 and the final C7 in the progression above, you'll hear the added minor seventh notes give them very different characteristics. The same thing works in minor keys (remember that the dominant chord is major in both major and minor keys). Here's a minor progression to look at:

Am | E7 | Am | C7 | F7 | Dm | E7 | Am

And a notated example based on that progression:

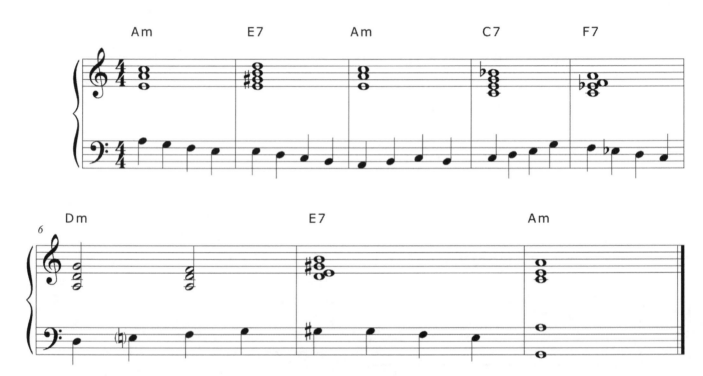

Again, the E7 chord has a very natural resolving effect. The C7 changes the feel of the piece to something more 'major' for a couple of bars, and the F7 sounds quite 'bluesy'.

Ninth (Major and Minor)
Form: 9 (D9, F9, E♭m9; sometimes Cmaj9, Fmaj9).

Ninths are interesting chords, used in lots of contexts. Basically, a ninth is a major or minor chord that has the note an interval of a ninth (14 semitones from the root) added. It comes in several different flavours and can have different effects in different inversions. It's sometimes taken to include the seventh as well – whether that's major or minor seventh. The chords below, for example, are both **major ninths**; you might see them notated as C9 and F9, but most careful musicians and composers would use

Cmaj9 and Fmaj9 to distinguish the fact that the seventh is major (i.e., that it's a major seventh chord with an added ninth; you might also see Cmaj7+9, Fmaj7+9 and so on):

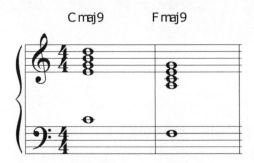

As you can probably see, this type of ninth usually needs two hands to play. A plain '9' is usually reserved for ninth chords that include a minor seventh:

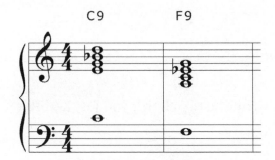

In a **minor ninth** chord the seventh is usually flat anyway, so you just add –m9:

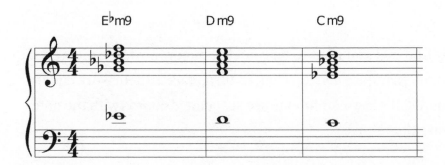

Meaty chords like this often sound great if they are arpeggiated (or 'spread'). That means playing and holding the notes one at a time, from bottom to top, until you're playing the full chord, instead of hitting them all simultaneously.

Next important point: in practice, ninth chords often omit the seventh – major or minor. In cases like that, the ninth is often incorporated next to the root note, effectively as an added second to a standard chord (the ninth note of a scale is identical to the second). This form of ninth has a lovely rich, warm sound. As we'll see in Part 3, you often hear it in used in split chord accompaniments :

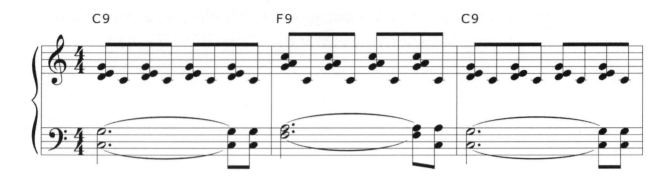

This can sound a bit jarring if you try it with minor chords, as the ninth and the minor third are right next to each other. Interesting effects are to be had, though, so it's worth experimenting. **Note:** you may sometimes see the chords above notated as –add2 (Cadd2, Fadd2, etc.) rather than as ninths.

Suspended Fourth[8]

Form: sus or sus4 (Csus, D♭sus4 – often pronounced 'C suss' or 'D flat suss four')

The suspended fourth is another 'does what it says on the tin' chord: you just add the note a perfect fourth (five semitones) above the root:

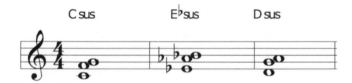

In major chords, you may find that you want to take out the major third to avoid a clash – that's what I've done in the examples above. That, in turn, makes them work equally well as major or minor chords. It's also common to see suspended chords with the notes separated by fourths rather than thirds:

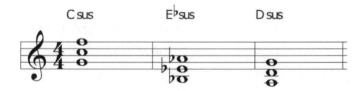

8. There's a video tutorial on both sus and 9th chords at:

www.jamcast.co.uk/piano-tutorial-adding-ninths-and-sus-fourths/

..it also touches on several techniques outlined in Part 3.

You can add a suspended fourth to more or less any chord, creating weird and wonderful sounds like E♭9sus:

Suspended chords have a close relationship with other chords like ninths. If you play Csus, you'll see it contains many of the same notes as G7sus; it's also a bit like some configurations of F9:

You can construct interesting chord sequences and riffs based around the interplay between suspended fourths and ninths – a technique that's been very popular since the 1970s, and remains so to this day:

Augmented (sometimes 'Augmented Fifth')

Form: aug or + (C+, Gaug, A♭aug, E+; 'aug' pronounced to rhyme with 'org'.)

Augmented chords are major chords that have had their fifth note (seven semitones above the root) raised by a single semitone. So, for example, Caug is C, E and G# - the original fifth, G, has been sharpened. The original fifth note is not usually retained:

A couple of interesting things to note before we talk about the uses of aug chords. First, you'll practically never come across a minor chord with an augmented fifth. To see why, consider the example of the C minor triad in its root position – C, E♭ and G. If you sharpened the fifth, G, by a semitone, you'd end up with C, E♭ and G#/Ab, which is effectively the same as a chord of A♭ in its first inversion, and would usually be written as such:

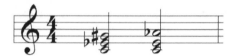

Second, although you can base augmented chords on (and name them after) any note, there are actually only four basic ones:

1.   Configurations of C, E and G# (Caug, Eaug and G#aug)
2.   "   "   D♭, F and A (D♭aug, Faug and Aaug)
3.   "   "   D, F# and B♭ (... you get the idea....)
4.   "   "   E♭, G and B

(Where a chord can have two possible names in the above – say, C#/D♭ – I've only used one of them for the sake of clarity).

Diminished Seventh

Form: dim or ° (Ddim, E♭°, A°. In general, writers who use 'aug' for augmented chords use 'dim' for diminished sevenths; those that use + for augmenteds tend to use ° for diminished sevenths. Note: some writers use dim and dim7 to distinguish between the diminished seventh and the diminished triad – which is the same chord minus the double-flattened seventh. In sheet music, 'dim' usually means 'dim7'.)

A diminished seventh chord is formed by taking a dominant seventh chord (see pp32-34) and lowering the third, fourth and seventh by a semitone each, while keeping the root the same. So here's C7 followed by Cdim7, in all inversions:

To save confusion that might be caused by all those flats, the accidentals are usually simplified:

Diminished sevenths are often used as passing chords in jazz and popular songs from the 30s, 40s and 50s. They are often heard today in music for film and TV – like augmented chords, they have a rather edgy, mysterious sound – but they are pretty rare in modern popular songs, which tend to have less complex chord sequences than the jazz-influenced pop of half a century ago.

In common with augmented chords, there is only a limited number of diminished sevenths – Cdim7 contains the same notes as E♭dim7, F#dim7 and Adim7 and so on, according to this pattern:

1. Configurations of C, E♭, F# and A (C°, E♭°, F#°, A°)
2. "   "   D♭, E, G and B♭
3. "   "   D, F, G# and B

Minor
Form: m (Am, Em, G#m)

A basic chord which, when played as a triad in its first inversion, includes a root, a minor third (three semitones above the root) and a perfect fifth (four semitones above the minor third). You can also add a second root note, an octave above the first:

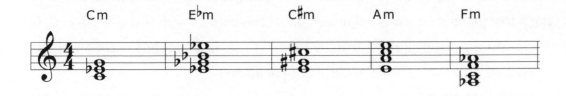

Apart from the minor third, basic minor chords can be inverted and voiced like basic major chords in every respect (see above). Although major chords and keys are sometimes simply known by their letters ('this is the chord of C', 'we'll sing this in B flat') minors always have the word 'minor' added.

Minor Seventh

Form: m7 (Am7, Fm7, C#m7 – usually pronounced 'A minor seven' etc.)

The minor seventh is a minor triad with a minor seventh added. An easy way to think about it is as a dominant seventh chord with the major third flattened. So, for example, to form Cm7 take C7 and flatten the E:

As we noted on p32, a minor seventh chord is usually identical in terms of its notes to a corresponding major sixth (Dm7 contains the same notes as F6; Cm7 the same notes a E♭6, and so on):

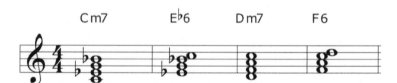

The way the chord is described is usually based on the context of key and inversion. If the minor seventh is built on the tonic chord of the key, it usually goes by the minor seventh name – i.e., Am7 would usually be called Am7, and not C6, in the key of A minor. Where neither the sixth nor the minor seventh is based on the tonic chord of the key, the name usually depends on inversion. If the chord C – E – G – B♭ has C, G or B♭ as its lowest note, the chord is usually named Cm7; if E♭ is the lowest note, it is usually called E♭6 – as you can see in the example above.

   Don't worry if that sounds excessively technical. Understanding it isn't critical for now, and it's something you'll begin to grasp instinctively as you get used to playing these chords in practice.

As we saw in the section on ninths on p41, minor seventh chords can be extended to minor ninths by adding the note a major third above the minor seventh:

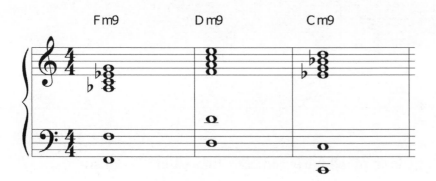

Less common chords

The chords listed above are by no means the only ones available to you as a pianist. Virtually any combination of notes you play can be described as a chord, though sometimes the more complex ones are difficult to define and are written in a variety of ways. If you get into jazz piano, in particular, you'll come across quite a few pretty weird chord names – E♭6/9, Fmaj7+, Gm9sus4. In general, these are all compound chords made up of the basic ones listed above. You'll also come across 11ths and 13ths – which, as you might correctly conclude, are just like ninths but with added notes at even higher intervals. However, in most popular music, chords like this are unusual.

If you're interested in jazz, it's also useful to know a bit about so-called *altered* chords. The term 'altered' is properly used for a type of seventh – you'll might see symbols like A7alt – but tends to get used as a general catch-all for chords that have been played around with, typically with flattened thirds, fifths and sevenths, and added ninths or fourths, to create a jazzier sound. For example, if you gave a jazz pianist a sequence of chords that looked like this:

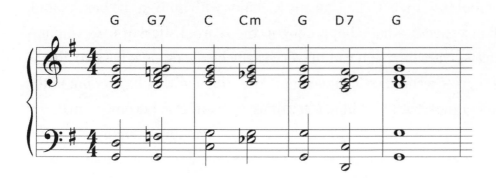

He might alter them so they looked a bit like this:

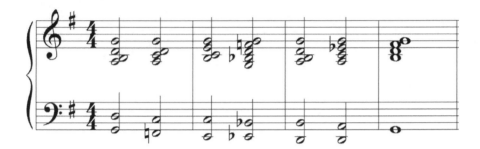

As you can see, the harmony is changed fairly radically there, but it's not so far away from the original that the same melody couldn't run over the top. Some of the theory behind altereds gets pretty complicated, and they can be difficult to notate. If you're interested in jazz harmony, there are some good books available on the subject, including Bill Boyd's *Jazz Chord Voicing* series.

A note on bass voicings

On the subject of voicings, it's worth taking a few moments to look at the issue of bass voicing, because it can make a big difference to the sounds of different chords. Play through this quick example:

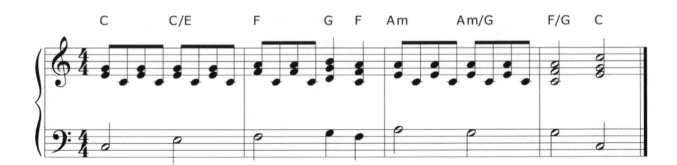

When a chord symbol is written 'C/E' it means 'C major with an E in the bass' – and, as you can see, that's exactly what's happening in the score. Different bass voicings have different effects. One thing you can do very easily by changing a bass voicing is give a feeling of progress or harmonic movement. You can hear that happening in the first and third bars of the example, where C becomes C/E and Am becomes Am/G.

Another very common bass voicing effect is the creation of complex dominants, some of which we saw on pp24-25. Basically, you can create a chord that has a dominant effect by combining the fifth note of the key's scale in the bass with the IV or IIm7 chords. As you can see in the example above, I've got an F with a G in the bass, which resolves very neatly on to C. The IIm7 would be Dm7 with a G in the bass (F6 would work just as well, as would Fmaj7). As usual, the best advice is to experiment with these chords and see what sounds you can come up with.

Developing your skills

It's all very well understanding the technical underpinnings of harmony, but as you charge through *Layla* or *Great Balls Of Fire* you can hardly stop to work out the theory behind the chord progressions.

Clearly, you need to get to the point where harmony becomes second nature - where the memory of what chord change works in what particular place lives in the tips of your fingers rather than in your overworked, accident-prone, conscious brain. You're not going to get there by staring at a page and memorising chords in different keys. You're only going to do it by playing the piano - a lot.

You may remember that in the introduction (specifically, on p8) I suggested getting hold of some popular songbooks. This is where they are going to really come in handy. Even if you don't much like the style of music in them, fiddle around with some of the songs and work out how the chords relate to the melody and the written score. It doesn't matter if you don't have the confidence to play this material through at this stage – just experiment with it and get a feel for how the chords work. Doing this sort of experimentation with other people's music is probably the single best way to get an instinctive understanding of chords and chord progressions. We'll look at some specific tips on how to do this in a moment.

More broadly, there are three techniques you can make use of: **experimentation**, **exploration** and **repetition**.

Experimentation is, in some ways, the simplest of the three. Sit at the piano, perhaps with some of the chord charts in this book in front of you, perhaps with some chord-marked sheet music. Play around: accustom yourself to the sounds of different chord in different keys. How does E♭ followed by A♭ followed by Gm7 sound?

Construct some short sequences of your own. Don't worry about perfection – just pursue the sound, and, when you start to hear a natural 'next chord' in your head, try to find it with your fingers. Use the information on chords above, and the resources in Appendix 1, to work out the identities of chords you've come across but can't name.

Remember that some chords can have ambiguous identities: the same chord can be both B♭6 and Gm7 in the same key (see p32, above). It will get its name according to context, inversion and the whim of the songwriter, composer or arranger.

Swap around from key to key, using minor and major and a range of the different keys within the two main groups. Can you transpose a chord sequence from F major to A major? Can you adapt it into B♭ minor? Working in different keys like this will help prevent you from getting stuck in the rut of playing in just a few familiar keys all the time. This is quite a common weakness in pop pianists, and you'll often meet people who begin to struggle outside keys like C, F, G and Am.

Nobody's saying you have to achieve equal levels of perfection in every key – unless you become a session musician, you'll rarely encounter situations where you want or need to play in B major or F# minor: in most amateur settings even the fussiest singer can shift up or down a semitone from awkward keys like these. Even so, it pays to be flexible. Regular scale practice is useful, but it will only take you so far. Sitting down and experimenting with patterns of chords in a variety of keys will make the biggest difference.

Exploration is all about playing around with other people's music to see how it fits together. If you talk to skilled pop pianists, a common theme emerges: many of them, when they were learning, branched out from the mainstream syllabus of classical pieces they studied for their exams and looked at other music.

Myself, I remember buying a book of songs taken from Disney films about the same time I joined my school jazz band. At first I didn't understand the chord symbols above the melody line. Once jazz practice had helped me work out what the symbols meant, I began to get a sense of where the chords went and what they did. Instead of playing the left hand and right hand of my Disney songs as notated, I started just playing the chords, and humming the tune over the top. After a while, I started playing the chords in the left hand and the melody in the right. Gradually I started putting together my own 'head' arrangements, using pretty much the same process as I'll describe in Part 3, for working with lead sheets.

The point is this: while I was playing like this, I was internalising a sense of which chords went where. If I played E♭, my fingers began to fall naturally on to Cm7 or Fm7 (two chords which might commonly follow E♭ in a progression). I noticed how chords shared notes, and how it didn't take much more than a change of emphasis or inversion, or a move to a different bass note, to change an E♭maj7 (say) into a Gm, or a Cm7.

Classic Broadway songs by people like George Gershwin, Richard Rodgers and Cole Porter are particularly useful for this kind of thing. Why? Because those guys were good theoreticians and composers (seriously good in Gershwin's case – he crosses the boundary between 'pop' and 'classical') and they employ rich, smooth, precise chord progressions in their work. Even if it's your ambition to spend your life playing Elvis covers, you can learn a lot from Gershwin and his peers. Play through their progressions, transpose them into different keys, experiment and see how they did things.

And **repetition**? Again, this is about giving yourself time; you need to work on harmony for long enough that it becomes instinctive. It should be a pleasure. When I was learning, I spent a lot of my time at the piano doing nothing more than tinkering around; I must have played the chord sequence C → C7 → F → Fm → C → G7 -→ C about ten thousand times, just because it appealed to me. I played it at different speeds and in different styles; I tried Fm7 instead of Fm; I used weird altered chords like Dm9$\flat$5 with a G in the bass[9] instead of G7. I internalised how harmony works.

---

9. You won't come across these that often outside of jazz, but $\flat$5 indicates that the fifth note of the chord (as played in root position) is flattened by a semitone. So Dm9$\flat$5 would consist of D, F, A$\flat$ (the flat fifth), C and E. The other note that is occasionally flattened in chords in this way is the ninth.

2: Improvising 12-Bar Blues

Even if you're not a big fan of the genre, learning some 12- bar blues is one of the fastest ways of developing your improvisation skills and getting used to playing songs in a variety of keys.

12-bar is also a useful skill because so much modern music, from jazz and rock'n'roll to hip hop and bluegrass, has its roots in the blues. Working on the blues will help reinforce some of the lessons of the last chapter, because you'll get a feel for the chords that make it up - the crucial tonic, subdominant and dominant (I, IV, V) that are the building blocks of western music from Bach to Coldplay. It also offers a route into basic improvisation techniques that you can use across genres.

The structure of 12-bar blues

There are several variants on the 12-bar sequence, so let's start off by looking at three of the most common ones, below. We're going to work on the basis of a twelve-bar in 4/4 time in C major. Any key can be used, although, as we'll see, once you start playing classic blues the difference between major and minor becomes more or less irrelevant. The chords for the most common 12-bar look like this in C:

C | C | C | C | F | F |
C | C | G | F | C | C |

(If you like, you can include a second G chord in the final bar to take you neatly back to the start of the progression. This would typically be done by either splitting the final bar into two beats of C and two of G, or making all four beats G).

To get an overall feel for the progression you could just play the basic triads, four to a bar, like this:

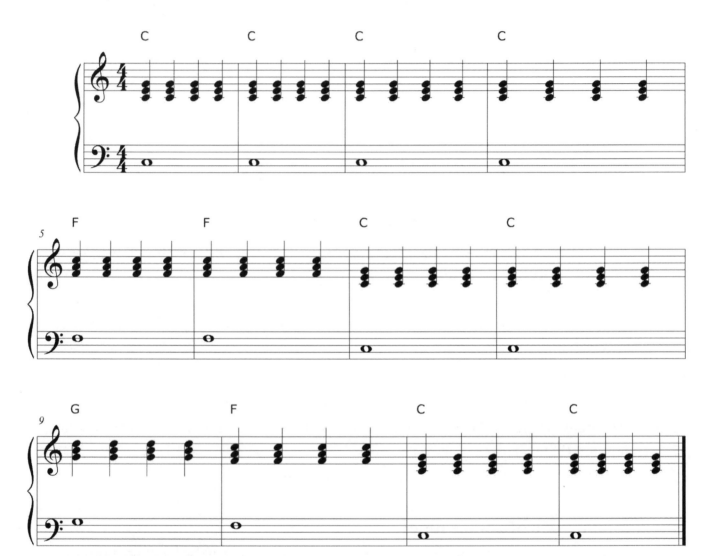

If you need reminding of the chord shapes, don't forget you can check the full charts in Appendix 2. If you're a bit more confident with chords, try playing around with different voicings and inversions.

If you play through that sequence, you should hear the relationships between the chords very clearly. The progression starts on C – the tonic chord – and moves back and forth between C and F before eventually journeying as far out as G, the dominant, before returning to C. Notice that the final resolution isn't G→C, but rather G→F→C. This IV-I resolution (an 'imperfect cadence') is very common in the blues, and indeed in its descendants - jazz, rock and much contemporary pop music.

If you're unsure of the role and use of dominant sevenths in harmony, this is a good opportunity to experiment. If you turn all the chords - Cs, Fs and Gs - in the sequence into sevenths (see pp21-22 and p32) you get some interesting effects. First, you'll notice how a G7 in the final bar offers a much stronger resolution back to the tonic than a plain G.

However, if you also turn the Cs and Fs into C7s and F7s you'll end up with a very bluesy effect; play through the sequence using C7, F7 and G7 instead of C, F and G, and you'll hear the sound I mean. This use of sevenths on chords other than the dominant of the key is a very common feature of jazz, blues and a lot of rock'n'roll. Here's a very simple, notated example similar to the one on the previous page. Listen out for those really 'bluesy' C7s and F7s and the enhanced resolving effect of G7→C:

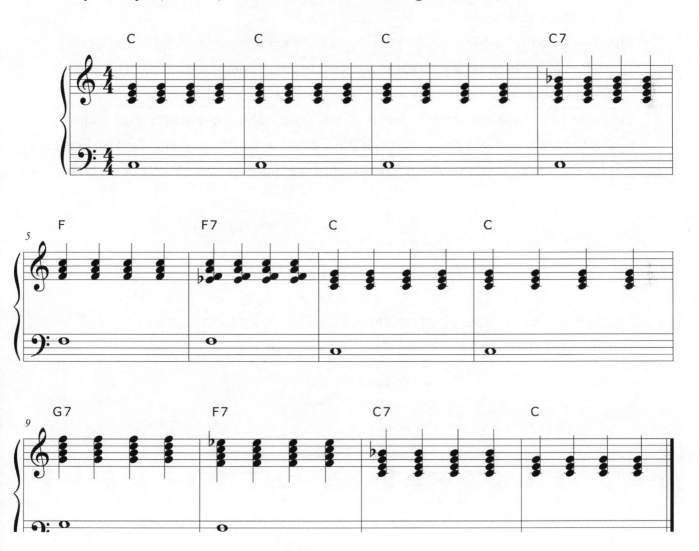

Standard 12-bar (variation)

This is a simple variation on the standard 12-bar pattern above, with the second C being replaced by an F:

C | F | C | C | F | F |
C | C | G | F | C | C, G...

As you can see, it's not that different. I've included a G in the last bar as an example of how you might indicate the end of one 'verse' and get yourself to the start of the next.

'New Orleans' 12-bar

The New Orleans 12-bar is relatively rare outside traditional jazz and blues, but it's worth looking at because it uses some interesting harmonies that can teach us quite a lot about how chord resolution works. In this instance, unlike the progressions above, I'm going to include the seventh chords. If you want to hunt out some songs that use this progression or slight variations on it (they aren't as common as standard 12-bars) you need to listen to some classic New Orleans blues such as *Basin Street Blues* or *Tin Roof Blues*.

C | F7 | C | C7 | F7 | F7 |
C | A7 | D7 | G7 | C, C7, F, Fm | C, G...

And here's a very simple interpretation of that sequence to save you the trouble of looking up all the chords if you're not sure about them:

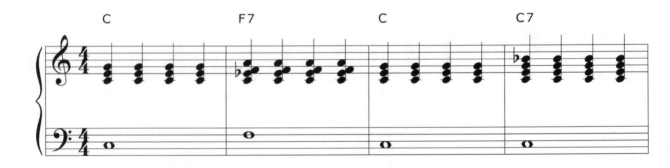

Play through the progression a few times to get a feel for it, referring to Part 1 and Appendix 2 if you need help with the chords. Some points to consider:

• Not all bars have just one chord in them. For example, if you look at bar 11 here, it contains four – C, C7, F, Fm (a very common 'closing' sequence, and in fact a bit of a cliché, in blues, traditional jazz and early rock'n'roll). Each chord has one beat. If there were two chords listed for the bar – as there are in the final C, G bar – you could usually assume that each chord has two beats. Sometimes you'll come across bars that contain two or more chords which share the beats unevenly – for example, the first chord might carry three beats and the second chord only one. This usually happens when the second chord is a passing chord:

C, Cdim7 | Dm7...
1,2,3......4

In cases like that, the beats are usually marked using strokes or numbers under the chords – *if you're using a chord chart and nothing more*. If you're using a lead sheet (see Part 3) that has both chords and melody, you're usually left to deduce how many beats each chord has from the spacing and its relation to the melody line. It's usually not very difficult.

• Bars 8, 9 and 10 are taken up by an interesting resolution sequence that uses the so-called 'circle of fifths' to get back to C. From the chord of C in bar 7, the progression suddenly jumps to A7 (a chord that doesn't appear naturally in the key of C); A7 is the seventh based on A, the major chord a fifth above D, and therefore naturally resolves on to D (or D7, in this case); D is a fifth above G, and G is a fifth above C. This is quite a rich sound that's common in traditional jazz. However, for our purposes it's a good way of demonstrating that chord progressions can move a long way outside their original keys, and even employ 'dominant'/ 'tonic' (V -> I) resolutions from completely different keys, but still come back to the original tonic quite comfortably.

Building blocks for blues improvisation[1]

Now that we know a bit about the structure of 12-bar, we're going to look at some of the very basics of improvisation – key principles not just for the blues, but for all kinds of genres.

Left hand independence

The first thing to deal with when approaching any kind of piano improvisation is the issue of your hands. You have two of them, and they both need something to do. This is what makes improvising on the piano consistently more difficult than any other instrument. You need to address the issue of what you're going to do with your left hand from the start, and to train it to do things independently of your right hand. Of course, all piano playing involves a bit of work on hand independence, but when you're improvising the problem becomes more challenging.

Challenging, but not impossible. When you look carefully at piano improvisation in most genres, you'll find that the relationship between the two hands is usually in one of two states:

1. The two hands are playing similar shapes/patterns. This is usually the case when you're playing in a band, or accompanying a singer. This style of playing - known as 'comping' - usually involves quite a few block chords. We'll look at this technique in more detail in Part 3.

---

1. You can find a series of three blues piano video tutorials on my website, mirroring the techniques described in this chapter. The first one is at:
www.jamcast.co.uk/learn-blues-piano-the-basics-part-1/
All the tutorials are indexed at www.jamcast.co.uk/book.

2. The left hand is creating harmony/rhythm to support the right. This is usually what you do when you're playing solo, or your piano is the leading instrument in an ensemble. The right hand does the creative stuff, perhaps carrying a tune, while the left backs it up, helping to create the rhythm and thicken the harmony. A classic example of this kind of left-hand work is the 'stride', which we'll also look at in Part 3.

It's the second kind of left-hand work that is most difficult. If you're working hard creating interesting figures, melodies and riffs with your right hand, how are you supposed to think about what you're doing with your left? The answer is twofold. First, a really deep, instinctive understanding of harmony is essential (so keep playing around with those chord patterns and progressions we met in Part 1, training your ear and your fingers). Second, you can use a degree – but just a degree – of automation in the form of pre-prepared patterns.

The great thing about 12-bar-blues on the piano, and one of the key reasons we're looking at it in this chapter, is that it allows you to improvise freely without having to worry too much about your left hand. The default setting is to use a fixed pattern in the left; you can break out from it occasionally, but it's a comfort zone you can return to more or less instantly.

Building left hand patterns

Let's look at some left/right patterns and examples you can use to begin to get an instinctive feel for 12-bar improvisation. As I've said, a typical approach is to use a fixed pattern in the left hand. In the context of classical music this would be referred to as an *ostinato*. Here are some examples, all in the key of C. The first is very 'straight':

The second has more of a swing:

While the third is more suited to up-tempo, boogie-woogie style blues:

There are hundreds of variations of bass lines like these, and it shouldn't be long before you have the confidence to develop your own. For now, though, we'll focus on building up our skills by focusing on just one of them in an exercise that's great for getting hands working together:[2]

2. You can see the exercise played in the video tutorials I mentioned in the footnote on p52. It starts at about seven minutes into the first video. Note for purists: yes, this exercise would arguably be better set in 12/8 time. I've used 4/4 here because that's the more traditional blues time.

If you play that exercise one hand at a time it's fairly easy, if a little bit boring. However, as you'll soon discover, playing it with hands together can be teeth-gratingly difficult, because you're asking left and right hands to do very different things: this is the blues equivalent of rubbing your tummy and patting your head at the same time. Master it, though, and you're well on the way to building a strong framework of hand independence for your improvisation.

Blues harmonies and the blues scale

Once you've grasped the basics of blues structure, it's time to think about how to make your blues musically interesting with richer harmonies and melodies. In this section we're going to look at some of the styles and sounds associated with the genre.

As I said in Chapter 2, sevenths are a key feature of blues harmony and improvisation. In general, the minor/flattened seventh is a defining sound of the blues – as are the flattened third and the flattened fifth. Here's a classic blues scale, in C. It's just like C major, but the third, fifth and seventh have been flattened.[3]

(Note that I refer to the key simply as 'C' rather than 'C major' – in this form it's actually closer to C minor, though, as we'll see, neither 'minor' nor 'major' really make sense).

Although I call that a classic blues scale, it might make more sense to call it a theoretical blues scale. The one that pianists usually use also includes the unflattened third and fifth (major third and perfect fifth), like this:

That is almost a chromatic scale – i.e., one that uses all twelve notes, white and black, between the two Cs. The only notes missing are the flat second (D♭), the flat sixth (A♭) and the major seventh (B). The first two sound a bit left-field even for blues - though

3. We briefly met flattened fifths at the end of the last section. In general, the terminology can be a bit confusing, not least because it differs between classical and popular musicians. If a jazz musician, for instance, talks about a 'flattened seventh' (or, more likely a 'flat seventh') he means a minor seventh. A flat third is a minor third, while a flat fifth is properly known as a *diminished fifth* (a standard, 'perfect' fifth can't be major or minor). A flat second is the same note as a flat ninth. If this seems utterly mind-boggling (and it beats me how anyone understands the ins and outs of music theory, least of all me) you can take consolation from the fact it's useful knowledge, but not essential for day-to-day playing. The stuff on intervals (thirds, fifths, sevenths, etc.) is explained in Appendix 1.

you can use them as passing notes in improvisation – and the major seventh sounds too mellow and cool for blues, which, again, isn't to say you can't use it if you really want to. By the way, you can find a listing of blues scales starting on every note of the 12-note scale in Appendix 1.

As you can probably see, the blues scale contains elements of both major and minor scales. If you listen to a piano blues it can sometimes sound major, sometimes minor, and sometimes somewhere in between. Play through the example below to see what I mean. If you can't manage the left hand together with the right, play the right by itself – it doesn't matter how slowly. It should demonstrate the major/minor ambiguity I'm talking about:

Is that in C major, C minor, both, or neither? As you'll also see from that example, another characteristic of the blues sound is its apparent discordance – which also contributes to the key ambiguity.

Grace notes

Grace notes are common in the blues and a lot of other improvised music. Pop pianists often call them 'crush' or 'crushed' notes rather than use the classical term. Also, in contrast to the classical approach, they are played with the same finger where possible – in this example, you'd put your finger on E♭ and slide immediately on to the E:

That would be regarded as poor style for a classical pianist, but it's important to remember that the qualities that are important to the classicist – smoothness, elegance, evenness – are less relevant to the blues. Of course, it's not always possible to slide like that. If you were playing in the key of E rather than C, the minor third→ major third transition would be G (natural) to G#, a white note to a black note. In that instance, you'd have to use two fingers. The major third/minor third crush is an integral part of blues piano because it's the closest one can get to an authentic 'blue note' - the bluesy tone that lies between the minor and major thirds. Singers, string and woodwind musicians can reach it by 'bending' a note, but it is impossible for pianists to play.

Rhythm

The blues, in common with jazz and a few other genres, makes heavy use of 'swung', syncopated rhythms. They are often represented like this:

However, the dotted quaver-semiquaver (or dotted crotchet-quaver) notation doesn't capture the feel of a swing quite accurately – the dotted crotchet is three times longer than the semiquaver. The actual feel of a swung rhythm is more closely represented by tying a crotchet and a quaver (or a quaver and semi-quaver) together as a triplet:

This is much closer to a true 'swing', because the first note of each pair is only twice the length of the second note. However, writing all those triplet brackets is a bit of a pain, and can make music look fussy. Therefore, jazz composers and arrangers usually use the dotted crotchet/quaver combination and assume you'll have the musical sense to play them as a swung pair, rather than exactly as written. That's the assumption I've made when scoring the examples that follow.

Right hand improvisation

Now you've thought about 12-bar structure and learned some options for your left hand, it's time to think about creating improvised melody in the right hand.

Improvisation isn't as scary as you might think. Yes, when you improvise on the piano you are 'making it up as you go along' and the exact mental process that involves is quite difficult to describe – largely because, once you've got the hang of basic improvisation in a particular style, it quickly becomes a subconscious, instinctive skill.

In fact, it's difficult to control your improvisations with nothing but your conscious mind unless you're going very, very slowly, because your brain just isn't fast enough to make rational decisions about which note should follow which. The secret lies in training your fingers to 'think' ahead of your brain and having a grab-bag of pre-practised runs and patterns ('riffs') that you can drop in at any one time. First of all, we're going to teach those fingers to think about melodic improvisation based on the blues scale.

We'll create a basic 12-bar based on one of the left-hand patterns we looked at above:

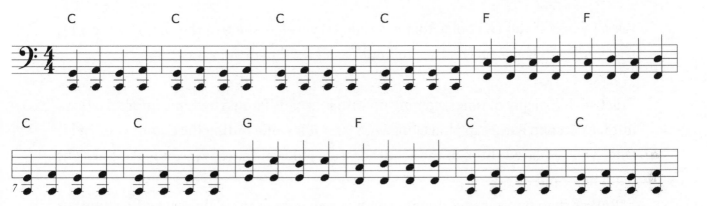

Play through a full 12-bar sequence with the left hand, just to get it firmly fixed in your head. Then play it again – only this time you're going to add some right hand. All you need to do with that right hand is play rhythmic patterns on one note – middle C. Focus on creating swinging, jazzy rhythms with it. Play it loud, play it soft, but stick to that one note. Here's an example of a possible improvisation you might come up with:

/cont...

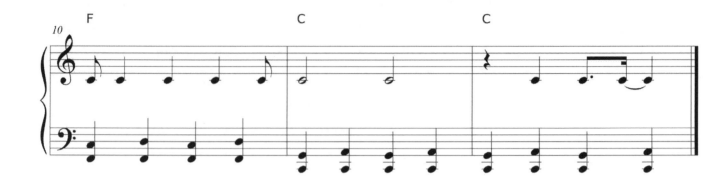

(Don't worry if you can't play that example very well – some of the rhythms are a bit tricky to read. Focus on creating an improvised rhythm of your own).

Practise that plenty of times, coming up with lots of different rhythmic improvisations until it's second nature to plod along with your left while hitting the C with your right. Once you've played through the sequence, say, a dozen times, we can make the right hand more interesting.

Rather than improvising rhythms on just one note in the right, try adding another note of the blues scale – E♭. Run through again, plenty of times, improvising rhythms and patterns with just those two notes. Don't worry about the fingers you're using; first and third are probably the natural choices, but it doesn't matter too much. In fact, you'll probably benefit by varying the fingers you use.

This time, a typical improvisation might look like this:

Again, run and run and run with it. Try using different fingers for the two notes – thumb and third, second and fourth, third and fifth. As I said above, precise fingering isn't that important in the blues, but it's good to get all your fingers used to 'thinking' for themselves. You may also have noticed the E♭ / E natural crushed note I slipped into the fourth bar.

When the C-E♭ combination is really firm, add an F. If you're feeling really con-

You'll notice in the last example I started jumping around between octaves in the right hand. Next, try combinations C-E♭-F-Gb-G in the right hand. Keep building up until you're confident about using the whole 12-note blues scale in your right hand. Some points worth noting:

• This will take time. If, practising the process described above, you end up playing the 12-bar sequence several thousand times, you're doing it exactly right. Patience and application are the secrets here: deal with these processes until they become second nature. That's the root of all improvisation – not just the blues.

• As you start incorporating more notes of the blues scale, you'll begin to notice that some work less well against certain chords. The most obvious example is the minor seventh (B♭), which doesn't like being played as a prominent note against the chord of F. As a passing note it's fine. Again, internalise what works and what doesn't.

• After you've really got the hang of this in C, try it out in other keys, starting with F, B♭ and G. Work out the 12-bar pattern and the appropriate blues scale (or look it up from the list in Appendix 2) and really go for it. Again, the secret lies in hundreds or thousands of repetitions.

Adding chords in the right hand

If you've gone through the above process thoroughly, you should now be confident about playing a simple blues with two hands. So far, I've only talked about playing single notes in the right hand. If you practise this process as much as I suggest you should, it won't be long before you begin to get more adventurous and start playing a couple of notes at a time, or even block chords. Let's look at how that might work:

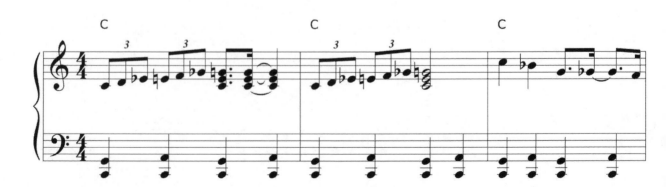

When you incorporate chords like this, you can begin to introduce some interesting sounds – ninths, for example:

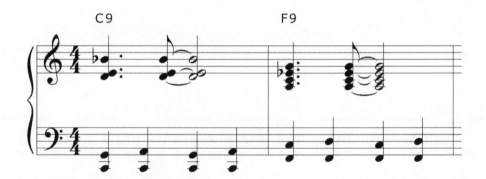

Riffs

As I said above, one of the secrets of improvisation is to have a mental bank of ready-made phrases and 'riffs' - simple, repeated patterns that you can slot in more or less anywhere. You should do your best to work up your own riffs, but to get you started here are a few examples of my favourites, in a couple of different keys:

It's worth noting that some riffs work better in some keys than others, especially if you're using a lot of crushed notes. For example, the third example works well in E, but would be a struggle in C; vice versa for the first example; the second could work in either key. Once you've got the hang of riffs, integrating them into your improvisation isn't very difficult. You can use them as 'safe havens' to retreat to when you're thinking about where to go next. In fact, a single riff can cover a whole 12-bar – a very common technique in fast rock'n'roll piano as played by people such as Jerry Lee Lewis:

Putting it all together

Where do you go once you've grasped the basics?

- Start using some of the other left hand patterns I suggested at the start of the section.

- Remember to use a variety of keys, focusing on C, F, G and B♭.

- Try working in some more exotic and unusual chords. Can you drop in some diminished sevenths as passing chords, perhaps using sequences like C→C#dim→F?

- Try faster and slower approaches. Once a blues gets past a certain speed it becomes a boogie-woogie. A couple of great (if rather tiring) left-hands for boogies:

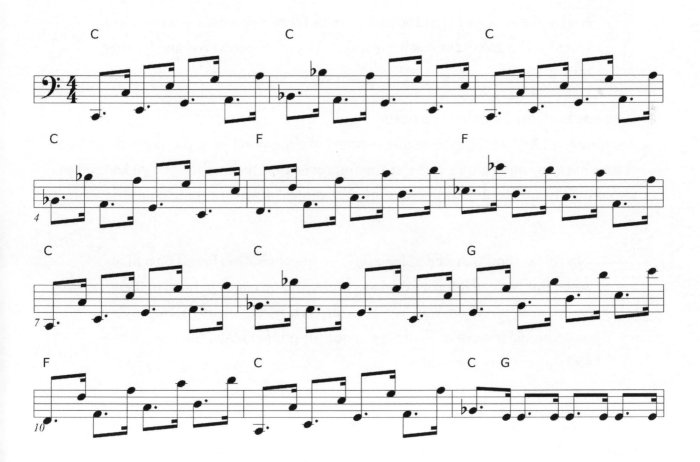

Notice the repeated G at the end of both those sequences – a common blues and boogie technique for marking the end of one 'verse' and leading into another.

Improvisation in other genres

Assuming you've spent a reasonable amount of time practising the skills described above, how do you begin to transfer the improvisation techniques you've learned in the context of 12-bar blues into other musical genres? Here are some pointers:

• In this section we've been focussing on improvisation based on a blues scale. But you can improvise on any scale, and on combinations of them. So, for example, if you were working on a jazz piece you might improvise on a combination of an ordinary major (or minor) scale, the blues scale and one or more jazz scales.[4]

4. Since the 1940s jazz musicians have become very interested in scales outside the mainstream major and minor. In particular, modal scales (or just 'modes') lie at the heart of modern jazz. They are outside the scope of this book, but the book list in Appendix 3 contains some titles that you can use as a resource for them.

• As you move away from the blues, you'll have to focus a little more on creativity in the left hand – not all genres let you get away with the figured bass patterns you can use when playing blues. We'll look at some other bass techniques in the sections on lead sheets and comping in Part 4.

• Listen and watch. Although you should always aim to take your own direction and develop your own unique style when improvising, you can learn a lot from other pianists. Take a look at the list of recommended DVDs in Appendix 3. Focus on pianists in genres you're interested in and study what they are doing with their hands when they improvise.

• Keep practising. We'll take a more detailed look at the psychology of improvisation and practice in Part 4.

3: Lead Sheets and Comping

Lead sheets contain the melody line and chords of a song. They help you pick up new material quickly and create off-the-cuff performances. Comping involves using a lead sheet or a chord chart to improvise a piano part that accompanies other instrumentalists or singers.

Note: some of the notated examples below are quite complex. You can see them played - and watch me going through much of the rest of the material in this section - in a series of video tutorials I've posted on the web. Like the other videos, they are indexed at www.jamcast.co.uk/book. I've also included several examples of famous performances that can be found online, mostly at www.youtube.com.

How lead sheets work

Remember *We Wish You A Merry Christmas* from Part 1? Here it is as a lead sheet:

As you can see, it's very straightforward – just chords, melody and lyrics with no indication of how they should be played.

You can get hold of lots of lead sheets cheaply if you buy a *fake book*. These often contain hundreds or thousands of different tunes, and are designed for buskers, wedding and event musicians, and anyone else who needs a wide repertoire and gets a lot of requests. Fake books started out in the 1940s and 1950s as bootleg compilations of famous songs. These days they are published legally, but the name has stuck – you can buy them in most good music shops. They get that name because creating an impromptu performance from a lead sheet is sometimes known as 'faking' (you'll also hear it called 'busking', whether or not it's being done out on the street). I've included a recommended fake book in the book list in Appendix 3.

Using piano-vocal scores as lead sheets

Most music shops sell popular songs in piano-vocal score format - a piano part with added melody, chords and lyrics. Here's how *We Wish You A Merry Christmas* might look in P-V arrangement.

70

P-V scores are much more common than pure lead sheets. That's not a problem, because the 'vocal' line is effectively a lead sheet for the song, containing melody, chords and lyrics. If you understand how to improvise a performance from this information, you can ignore the piano arrangement altogether.

Let's imagine you've got hold of the piano-vocal score for a fictional song called *E Flat Lead Sheet*. The first eight bars look like this:

/cont...

71

har - mo - ny_____ and ly - rics that are wit - ty!_____

A sure-fire hit, if ever there was one. As you can see, it has melody, chords (including tablature markings for guitarists, which you can ignore) and a piano arrangement. If we mentally remove the lyrics and all the other material we don't need, we end up with something like this:

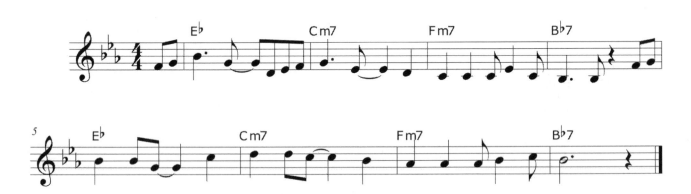

So how do you turn this into a piano performance? A good way to start is to get a sense of its structure and harmony by playing the melody in the right hand accompanied by block chords in the left, perhaps like this:

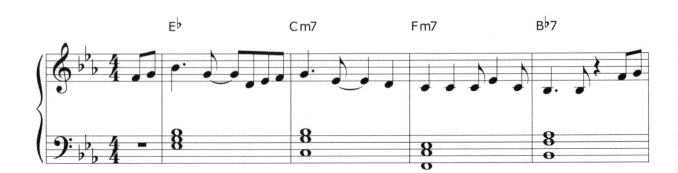

(You'll come across the term 'block chords' quite a lot in this chapter. I'm just using it to describe chords played in a straightforward way, with all notes sounding together, rather than chords that are split or arpeggiated – concepts we'll come to shortly. Remember, if you're unsure of any of the chords, a look-up chart of the most important ones can all be found in Appendix 2. If you need to remind yourself of any of the basic harmonic principles, you'll find them in Part 1.)

Now that the publisher's arrangement has been removed, we can see that this is a fairly ordinary chord sequence, starting on the tonic chord of the key (E♭) and finding its way to B♭ (the dominant) twice during eight bars. When you're playing through a lead sheet for the first time, it's a good idea to get a sense of the 'shape' of the chord progression like this, so that your brain has a reasonable idea of where your fingers are going to be heading.

You may be interested to know that the chord progression we're looking at here is very common, and can be found in many classic songs in various keys, including *Blue Moon* and *Heart and Soul*.

Making it more interesting

Of course, just playing the melody with chords isn't going to be very satisfying in most cases – the whole reason we use lead sheets is to unleash our creativity. Exactly where you go from here depends on the style of the music you're dealing with – something we'll come to in a moment. However, there are some general techniques you can apply to most styles:

• Thicken up the harmony in the right hand: instead of just using single notes, play a combination of melody and chords. You might play the right hand of *E Flat Lead Sheet* something like this:

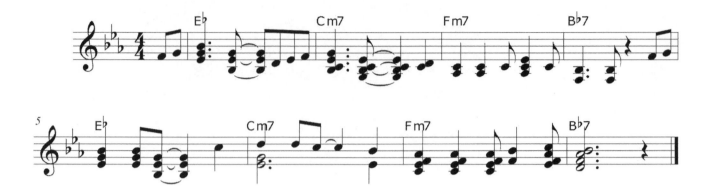

That may look much more complicated than the bare melody, but it's not really – all you're doing is filling in chords under the tune.

• Borrow bits from the publisher's arrangement. You can do this if you're playing from a P-V score, rather than from a pure lead sheet. Have a look at the publisher's arrangement and see if there are any distinctive or interesting motifs you can drop into your version.

• Create a clear bass line. Many commercial arrangements have rather thin bass lines. They are often very simple, or quite high. Here's the bass line from the P-V score piano arrangement of *E Flat Lead Sheet*:

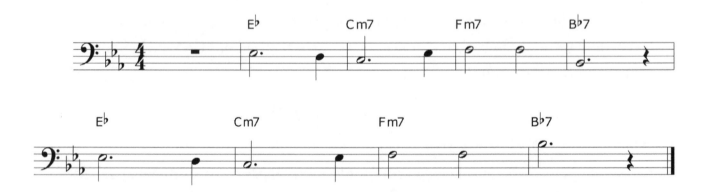

That's a common bass line style (we'll look at it again later) and not bad as far as it goes. However, if we want to, we can make it richer and more powerful without doing anything too technical. For example, we could add a bit more harmonic character and rhythmic drive by adopting a stride bass (a style we'll look at in more detail later):

Be careful about adding too much power in the bass, and, in particular, be wary of block chords more than an octave below Middle C, as they tend to sound unclear. Exactly how unclear depends on how low you go, and what type of piano you're playing. A quick solution is to avoid playing low bass notes together with the thirds immediately above them. Instead, stick to combinations at least a fourth or a fifth apart. These chords, for example, would sound quite muddy:

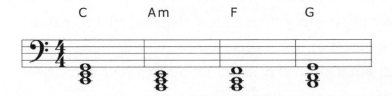

While these would probably be OK:

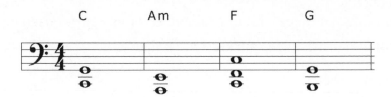

The extent to which you use the above techniques will depend on the type of songs you're performing. Also, if you're playing in a band, other instruments will join in the job of creating rhythm, bass line and harmonies, so you can ease off a little. If you're playing solo, or accompanying a singer, you have to do the all hard work yourself.

Fingers and pedals

Before we deal with different styles of music in lead sheet form, we need to take a look at what to do with your fingers and your piano's pedals.

Fingering

While good fingering is essential for classical playing, it's much less important for playing popular music. As a pop pianist you'll get on pretty well if you don't worry about fingering at all and just play the notes as they fall under your hands. If you have to deal with an awkward jump or run, dive on the sustain pedal to cover the gaps.

That's not to say that having a good fingering ability is worthless – far from it. One of the best reasons to continue (or resume) your classical playing is that it helps you develop an instinctive feel for good fingering - useful, if not essential, for pop playing.

Pedalling

Most pianos have two pedals: a sustain pedal on the right and a damper (soft) pedal on the left. Some have a third pedal in the middle. If you've got one, it's probably either an ultra-soft 'practice pedal', or else a *sostenuto* pedal, which is like a sustain pedal that only holds the notes that are played when the pedal is pressed.

Middle pedals are relatively rare, so we'll just deal with sustain and soft. Sustain is the most important: when you press it (on a real piano) it lifts all the dampers off all the strings, letting those that are played continue sounding until either their natural vibration stops or you lift your foot off. Digital pianos achieve the same effect electronically. The sustain pedal is great for creating rich, lush textures – it's a defining feature of the instrument in that respect. But it's also very useful for making your music flow smoothly, covering the gaps between jumps in hand position.

Exactly how you use the pedal is one of those areas of learning to play pop piano that is very instinctive. Ultimately, it's a question of resting the ball of your foot on the pedal and letting your ankle do the thinking – it takes a bit of trial and error as you get used to the effects, but competence comes surprisingly quickly. Quick tips:

> • On most pianos you don't need to depress the sustain pedal very far to lift the dampers off the strings – in fact, if you fully depress the pedal every time you use it, you can end up with a sustain effect that's clanky, stilted and tiring to maintain. Again, it's all about experimenting and finding out what you need to do on different pianos.

• Unless you're after particular effects, it's not a good idea to hold the pedal across chord changes, or for too long during a period of melodic movement, because you end up with a muddy mess. Once again, make a point of playing with your foot resting on the pedal and trust your ear to tell you when to push and when to lift.

• You'll often find yourself pedalling at the start of bars, or over chord changes, in a fairly rhythmic, 'pumping' way. Bear in mind that's not a technique to aim for consciously: it's just one way you might end up using the pedal. As usual, the best advice is to experiment and discover what works and what doesn't as you play.

The soft pedal is slightly different. It works in one of two ways, depending on the type of piano you're playing. On grand pianos – which typically have three strings per note and a hammer action based on a direct drop on to the strings – pressing the soft pedal moves all the hammers and the keyboard (which is a bit alarming when you first do it) a little to the right, so that only one or two strings are played. On an upright piano, the hammers are moved from their resting positions, slightly closer to the strings. Whichever mechanism is used, the resulting sound is quieter and more mellow.

If you're thinking of buying a digital piano, try to choose a more expensive model that has really good on-board piano samples. Cheap digitals mimic the effect of the soft pedal by just dropping the volume a notch or two: better ones have different samples for notes with and without the soft pedal.

Style and movement

Back to lead sheets. For the purposes of this next section we're going to divide twentieth century popular music into two very broad types: material written before the 1960s, and material written after the 1960s. In general, songs of each type demand a slightly different approach if you're working them up from a lead sheet – or indeed, comping them (on which subject, more later).

Type 1: Pop from the 30s, 40s and 50s, jazz standards and show tunes
This category covers jazz standards and swing; the work of composers like George Gershwin, Cole Porter and Richard Rodgers; the songs of performers like Frank Sinatra, Ella Fitzgerald and Bing Crosby; the majority of Broadway show tunes and quite a few early rock'n'roll ballads. The style is still popular in film and musical theatre, and

although jazz is the dominant genre within it, it's not universally jazzy. In some ways, these songs tend to be the easiest to perform from lead sheets. Although harmonies from this era sometimes appear complex - with lots of sixths, minor sevenths, augmenteds and so on - chord progressions and song structures are generally very regular. Additionally, the songwriters tended to be pianists, and songs written on the piano are usually more pianist-friendly than songs written on the guitar.

This type of music can work very well with patterned, easy-to-memorise bass lines. These include the full stride, which we saw above. It has its roots in ragtime and early jazz:

There's also the octave stride (which I call the 'bounce'). You play the upper note of each pair with your thumb and the lower note with your fifth finger:

And then there's the walking bass, which mimics the style of a jazz double bass:

So working from the lead sheet of a song from this era can be pretty simple: you thicken up the melody in your right hand, using the technique we looked at on pp73-74, above, while your left hand plays chords in pre-learned patterns. Starting with that basic approach, you can add variations, improvisations and extra harmonies, making your final performance as simple or as complex as you like.

Let's have a look at how you might take a song from this era and work it up from a lead sheet. Overleaf is a sample verse in lead sheet format. It's from a song called *The Real Thing*, a pastiche of the kind of tunes Frank Sinatra had huge success with in the 1950s and 1960s, and which had their roots in the big band style of the 30s and 40s.

The first thing to do is think about the left hand options open to us. Here are the first three bars, with the right hand just playing the melody and the left a stride bass:

The stride works quite well, and generates a good rhythm and harmonic accompaniment. But what if we want to play the song quite quickly? It's hard to play a stride very fast, and, when you do, it can sound a bit awkward. There's an alternative overleaf: the same right hand with an octave stride ('bounce') in the left, which is easier to play at a quick tempo:

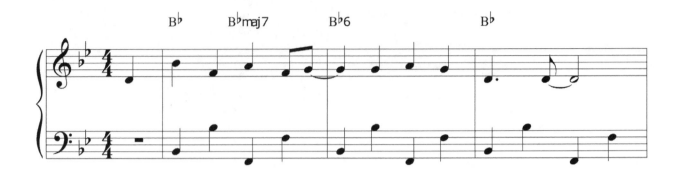

(You'll notice that the bouncing left hand in that example is written in crotchets, whereas the example on p78 was in quavers. In fact, if you were writing this piece from scratch to be very fast, you would probably notate it in 2/4 time with the principle notes as quavers rather than crotchets. I've used crotchets for ease of comparison with the stride bass example on the previous page.)

Next, let's look at it with a walking bass, a style that can add real energy and drive to quick songs. The walking bass also offers the benefit of being pretty easy, providing you have a good grasp of your scales:

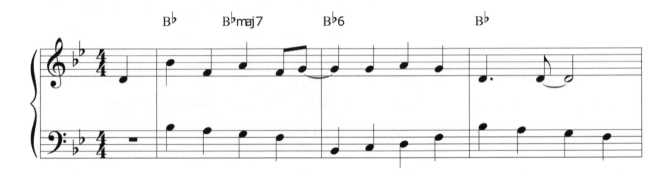

And, finally, here it is with a bass of block chords – this would work well if you were playing the song down-tempo or with a separate rhythm section:

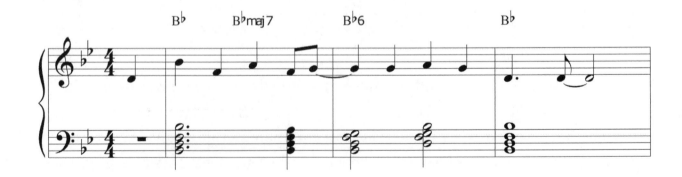

Notice that I've added a little bit of rhythmic variation in the bass rather than just holding each block for the full number of beats its chord occupies in the progression.

You'll find you get the very best results when you mix and match left hand patterns to complement what's going on in the right hand. So, for example, the bounce works very well in bars 1 to 8, but once we get to the E♭maj7 → E♭dim → Edim →Gm7 sequence that starts in bar 9, block chords add a bit of extra punch to the harmony:

If you have P-V scores for songs from this era, select a couple and practise some left-hand patterns based on their chord progressions, accompanied by the melody in the right hand. It'll be hard at first, but as you get used to it you'll find you begin both to combine the different styles and develop new ones of your own. If you work on this technique and take it far enough, you'll end up with interesting, composite, improvised left-hand patterns.

And what about your right hand? Here's an example of how you might develop a right-hand part for *The Real Thing*. First three bars:

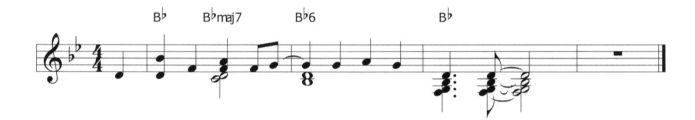

As we saw when we looked at a potential right hand for *E Flat Lead Sheet* on pp73-74, above, it's a case of thickening up the basic melody with the underlying chords. Once you've built some confidence, you can start adding improvised melodies as well: make sure you know the chord sequence well, then use the one note-two notes-three notes system we learned in Part 2 to build up improvisations over a left-hand bass. You can also develop the harmony a little. The classic, 'jazzy' way to do this is to add 6, 7, 9, maj7 and maj9 chords. You'll see that's what I've done in the example above, on the third beat of the first bar (adding a ninth to the B♭maj7 chord) and in the third bar (adding a sixth to the B♭ chords).

Slower songs from this era

You can use exactly the same techniques for dealing with slow, ballad-type numbers written in this kind of style. The 'bounce' bass technique begins to sound a bit creaky when you take it down to a slow tempo, but the stride and walking bass both work well with slow to moderate numbers. Very down-tempo numbers (I'm thinking of classics like *Misty* and *A Nightingale Sang in Berkeley Square*) work best with bass lines built on single notes and block chords. Take a look at some professional pianists playing this type of number to get a sense of what they do.

Listening and watching

If you have access to YouTube, take a look at some videos of pianists performing jazz, blues and pop tunes from the mid-century. You might check out Oscar Peterson, Dr. John, Hoagy Carmichael, Jools Holland and Jamie Cullum. They all have different styles, but the kind of movements and techniques they use reflect the left hand/right hand division we've been discussing above.

Type 2: Pop since the 1960s

I'm including rock, pop, country and contemporary folk in this category, and mainly focussing on relatively complex, ballad-type styles (which isn't to say they are all slow songs). You'll do well applying the techniques that follow to the works of performers like the Bee Gees, The Carpenters, Elton John, Carly Simon, Diana Ross and the less 'rocky' work of bands like Queen, R.E.M and Oasis.

Songs in this category are very different from the older, jazzier types of songs we discussed above. In some ways they are easier, but they can present some challenges.

• In general, chords are simpler and there are fewer of them than in older popular music.

• Quite a lot of pop from the past forty years is available in sheet music form, but usually in the original key it was written, which, more often than not, is a key better suited to guitarists than pianists. You'll find that familiarity with keys like G major, A major and E major comes in handy.

• Melodies can be surprisingly complex with quite a lot of dotted rhythms. Surprisingly, the 'jazzy' numbers we looked at above can be much more regular in contrast.

•Many up-tempo songs have been written with a full band in mind, and it can be difficult to mimic driving beats and bass lines on the piano. On the other hand, slow and medium tempo songs are often very easy to play.

• Most pop piano since the late 1960s has been based around the use of block chords, syncopated and 'rocked' against one another in a very close relationship. This is a contrast to older styles, where the left hand typically deals with rhythm and harmony, while the right carries the melody and improvisations on it.

• As such, there's much less use of patterned left hands than you see in music from the 1920s to the 1950s; in general, left hand parts are based on simple bass lines and block chords. There's a much greater emphasis on the two hands working together to create rhythm and harmony.

A classic example of many of these techniques in action is Elton John's *Song For Guy* – a modern pop piano piece where the right hand is making the play in terms of harmony and rhythm and the left fills in a fairly basic bass line.

Let's take a look at an example in detail. Here's an 8-bar verse section of a modern pop ballad called *Cruel Intentions*. It's written as a lead sheet with simple, publisher-type piano arrangement.

(Quick harmonic note. This is in E major, and normally the B-root chord in that key would be B or B7, the dominant. Here it's Bm7, giving an unusual effect, especially with the addition of the prominent E in the right hand.)

There's a wide variety of approaches we can take with a lead sheet like this. The easy thing to do is play block chords in the left and the melody in the right:

...which works OK, but is a little lifeless. Let's try thickening up the right hand with chords, just like we did with the older songs of the first type. This looks a bit complicated written out, but is relatively simple to play:

You'll notice that the fingers in the right hand that are responsible for the harmony notes are moving less than the top line fingers; typically you'll be holding on to chord notes with your thumb and index finger, while fingers 4 and 5 carry the melody – your middle finger (3) is split between the two roles. Also, notice the arpeggiation mark next to the Bm triad at the start of bar 5. As we saw in Part 1, an arpeggiated chord is 'spread', bottom to top, with all the notes played and held in quick succession until all are sounding. It's a very easy, natural action and can add a lot of movement and interest to piano improvisations.

Finally, we can add some interest in the bass. Syncopated bass lines that mimic the effect of a bass guitar are very common in this kind of style. For example:

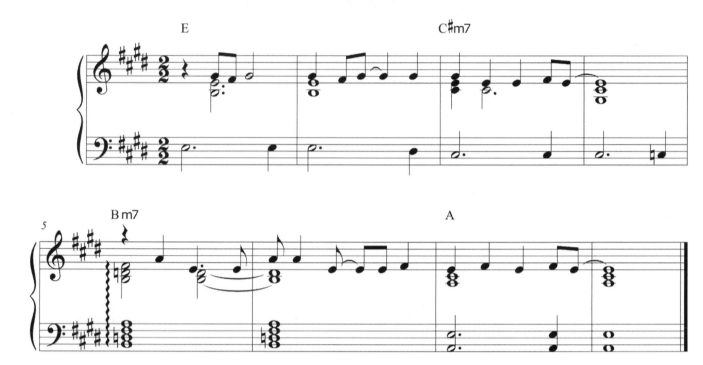

Look at the way rhythm is being created in that example. As we saw above, the approach with older, jazz-derived pop songs is usually to let the left hand define the rhythm, using a stride, bounce or walking bass in the absence of a band rhythm section. In the more modern style, the right hand has much more rhythmic responsibility while the left plays a simpler role. The movements of the two hands complement one another much more.

That's quite hard to grasp with only one or two examples and a written explanation. Search for some good performances on YouTube (specific suggestions on p92, or check out some of the DVDs listed in Appendix 3) and watch what skilled contemporary pop pianists do with their hands.

Comping

Comping (short for 'accompanying') is a slightly different skill from that of creating your own piano performances from lead sheets, but very closely related. Essentially, it's the way you approach a lead sheet (or raw chord sequence) in a situation where the piano doesn't have to carry the melody. So, for example, you would comp while playing in a band (unless you happened to be playing a solo), or while accompanying yourself or someone else singing.

If you like to sing while you play, being able to comp will make a big difference to the quality of your performance. Why? Because in most P-V arrangements the piano part follows the melody – in other words, if you follow such scores exactly, your right hand and your voice end up doing nearly exactly the same thing, which doesn't sound very professional. A basic ability to comp gives you a much slicker, more interesting sound. Better still, it's really not a difficult skill: at its simplest, all you're doing is playing the chords and adding some rhythm and texture. The basic secret of success is to get hold of a load of lead sheets or P-V scores and just play around with the chord sequences, starting simple and experimenting with added harmonies and different rhythms, voicings and inversions.

Even so, there are some specific techniques you can use. Let's go back to our two broad types of modern popular music and take a look at some examples to get you started.

Type 1: Comping pop from the 30s, 40s and 50s, jazz standards and showtunes
With pop music of this vintage, you have a number of options – most of them tied to tempo and whether you're playing solo or with a rhythm section.

If you're comping a fast song solo (i.e., without someone else playing bass and/or drums behind you) you could go for a patterned left hand with block chords 'stabbing' in the right. That's easier to notate than explain, so here's how you might comp along to *The Real Thing*, which we first met on p79:

Can you see what's happening there? The left is keeping the pulse going and creating a harmonic background while those stabbing chords in the right are adding extra harmony and contributing to the complexity of the rhythm. If you've mastered your patterned left hands and you know your chords, this approach is really pretty easy.

Comping a fast song with bass and/or drums behind you is even easier, because you don't have to worry about maintaining the beat with your left. Both hands can go for those stabbing chords:

Comping a slow song in this style, with or without a rhythm section, is all about rich, lush chords with lots of arpeggiation (spreading chords from bottom to top rather than playing all the notes simultaneously). If you're playing solo you can add a bit of extra movement and drive with your left hand. Here's an example, based on a chord sequence identical to the one in *E Flat Lead Sheet*, which we looked at earlier:

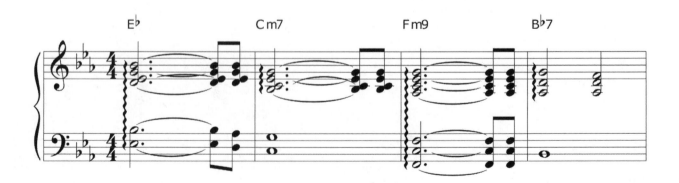

The usual advice applies: play around with different styles for different songs. If you like singing, sing along as you play, and see if you can accompany yourself. Don't be rigid: remember that if you're playing a stride or a bounce left hand, you don't have to play it all the way through a song: you could switch to block chords or a walking bass during a middle section, for example.

A good way to grow in confidence with these techniques is to take a few songs and learn them really well, to the point where you don't have think hard to remember which chord comes next in the progression. That way you can give your full attention to creating rich, interesting comps (or lead sheet improvisations for that matter, as the same principle applies to those).

Type 2: Comping rock, pop, country and contemporary folk
In more modern pop music, the classic piano comping technique is to take chords, break them up and improvise on them in a basic way with the hands working closely together. Here's an example of how you might do that with a typical chord sequence:

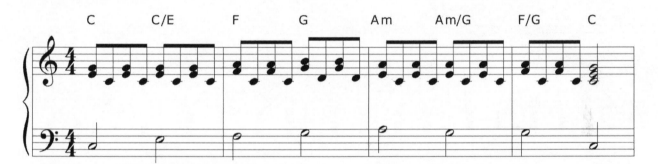

Those are split chords, and you may remember we looked at them briefly in Part 1. The technique of taking a triad, splitting it and rocking backwards and forwards between a pair and a single note is very common. It sounds effective, and it's easy for novice pianists to master quickly. You can hear it used in songs like John Lennon's *Imagine*, *Don't Look Back in Anger* by Oasis and *Rainy Days And Mondays* by the Carpenters. This basic technique, and variations on it, works really well for slow and medium-tempo songs.

Let's build on it a bit. One of the first things we can do is modify the chord sequence slightly by adding interesting extra harmonies. Ninths and suspended fourths work well. Overleaf is our example from p37 again:

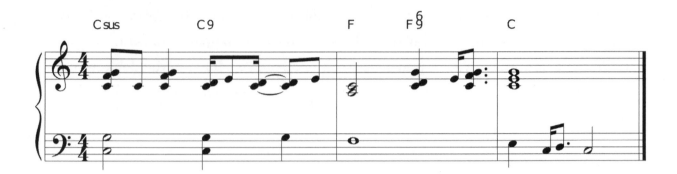

As you can see, that example also moves away from the regular rhythm of the one before it. It's more syncopated and has more of a sense of movement.

Below are a couple more examples of comps for slow to medium contemporary pop, each based on a fairly simple progression. Notice how, in each case, the rhythm and movement come from the interplay of the hands. In the first one, although there are some split chords in the right hand, we're mainly using blocks, with the two hands rocking against one another. Like many of the examples in this section, this needs a fair amount of sustain pedal to hold it together:

The next one is a bit more complicated (so don't forget you can watch it being played in the tutorials at www.jamcast.co.uk/book).

It still contains split chords, plus a few more twiddly bits. Notice I'm labelling it with straightforward chords (A, E and D), but actually playing both the E and the D with suspended fourths. On most lead sheets you often won't see chords listed with extra fourths, ninths and so on unless the additional notes are blindingly obvious in the melody line. That doesn't mean you can't take a chord and add these bits and pieces yourself to make it more interesting:

What about the bass? If you want to create a distinct bass line for comps like this, you can use the syncopated line technique, which we've already seen in various configurations in some of the examples above:

What that's basically doing is moving between the root notes of the different chords, mimicking the kind of thing a bass guitar would do in a band line-up. If you're including that line in your comping, after a while you'll find you have an urge to make it more complex and add more rhythm: go for it – it should be quite a natural process. The great thing about this method is that you can keep it relatively simple until you've mastered the technique.

If you're playing in a band with a bass instrument you won't need to worry about this left hand work quite so much, but if you're accompanying yourself or just one other singer/instrumentalist, it's invaluable.

Another good bass technique that works well for slower, unaccompanied, ballad-like numbers involves using arpeggios (broken chords), a bit like this:

Some examples

Here are three great examples of slow-to-medium contemporary comps (all available on YouTube at the time of writing):[1]

• Nerina Pallot's *Geek Love* is usually performed with piano and a full backing band, though she also does a version with just piano and vocal. The piano part is rich, but not at all complex – it's a beautiful example of how good comping can deliver strong rhythms and harmony while integrating seamlessly with vocals. Another good Pallot video is her performance of *I Don't Want To Go Out* – relatively minimalist comping, but very skilfully done.

• Elton John's *Tiny Dancer* is a classic. He uses lots of arpeggiated and split chords, and doesn't go down deep into the bass very often – but is very effective when he does. A very characteristic Elton John effect you can hear in performances of this song is the dynamic range of his piano parts: he'll go from loudish to soft very suddenly, without losing the rhythmic effect of his playing.

• As a complete contrast, watch Tori Amos performing *Winter*. It has considerable dynamic range, but at the start it's very delicate – listen to how the comp starts high on the piano and gradually adds depth.

But what if we're dealing with a fairly up-tempo song? The simple split chords approach we covered on p89 will serve you pretty well as the tempo increases, but you'll also find yourself using more block chords. If you can, have a look at some medium- and up-tempo piano pop on YouTube. Some suggestions:

• Ben Fold's *Landed* is an interesting song, because Folds uses the piano in several different ways: in the introduction he has his hands working together, before moving to comping split chords (a la *Imagine*) as he sings. Then, during the piano solo, he really attacks the bass to drive the song's rhythm. One of the things that makes Folds an interesting pianist

---

1. I've not included links to specific performances, as they change so often. However, you should be able to find all the songs listed in this section by using the YouTube search function. Several of the performers I've listed here have official YouTube channels (which should come up in the top results if you search their names). As well as high quality video of their songs, they often feature interview material. Nerina Pallot's is especially good:
  http://www.youtube.com/user/nerinapallottv

is the way he uses the piano as a percussion instrument – he really hits the thing. That's a pretty common technique among contemporary pop pianists, but Folds does it better than most.

• Another good example from Folds is *Not The Same*. The best version for seeing what he's doing on the piano is a video shot during a gig in Central Park, New York, in 2004.

• For pure, up-tempo rock'n'roll piano, check out anything by Jerry Lee Lewis. Although he's playing in a very different style from Ben Folds, he is also a very percussive player. There are lots of block chords in there, and usually a very simple patterned bass. Lewis also makes heavy use of the *glissando* - a long slide up or down the white notes of the piano. Despite his fame, Lewis isn't that brilliant a pianist; he's just taken the skills I outlined in Part 2 and learned to apply them very quickly, at top volume, and with a lot of showmanship thrown in.

While we're on the subject, 'glissing' looks impressive, and is actually very easy: if you're coming down the keyboard, use the thumb of your right hand so that the thumb-nail is catching the edge of each new note. Going up, turn your hand over and slide up using the nails on your middle three fingers. If you want to gliss on the black notes - which creates a pleasing sound based on the *pentatonic* ('five note') scale - flatten out your hand and use the fleshy undersides of your four fingers to 'smear' the notes, whether you're going up or down. The basic rule is fingernails for white notes, fleshy bits for black notes. Don't get those the wrong way round, or accidentally use your knuckles, as glissing mistakes can be quite painful.

Anyway, in each of those examples, the piano is played as a percussion instrument as much as a melodic one. The players aren't actually beating the thing (although Lewis comes close) but there are lots of stabbing, rhythmic effects in all the performances you might have looked at. As we saw when we looked at contemporary pop lead sheets on pp83-86, the right hands have lots of movement in them.

Vamps, loops and grooves

One other technique that's worth a mention is the use of a vamp, loop or groove. The three terms basically describe the same thing – a repeated piano pattern, perhaps four or eight bars long, played over and over underneath all or part of a song. 'Vamp' is the preferred term among jazzers, while comtemporary pop musicians tend to use 'groove' and 'loop'.

You can hear a classic jazz vamp in Nina Simone's *My Baby Just Cares For Me*. Simone doesn't play the vamp the whole way through, but it's very distinctive, and probably the most recognisable part of the song.

Grooves are very common in quite a lot of R'n'B, soul and (especially) funk. Have a listen to Stevie Wonder's *Superstition*. It's basically a heavily simplified 12-bar blues (pretty much based on the I chord all the way through, with a quick move on to V and VI at the end of every chorus). Performing live, Wonder plays a complex groove. The recorded version is every more interesting, because he plays a *series* of grooves, recorded separately and multitracked on top of one another in the studio to produce a rich, layered sound. The main instrument that Wonder plays on the recording isn't actually a piano but a clavinet – a kind of electric clavichord that's a distant descendant of the harpsichords and virginals of Renaissance Europe.

The term 'loop' tends to get used either in a recording context (i.e., an instrumentalist plays a pattern a few bars long, and it's digitally copied and repeated for all or most of the track – listen to Fat Boy Slim's *Praise You*) or when dealing with genres of pop outside the Afro-American tradition of the 60s, 70s and 80s. A classic example of a keyboard loop is in R.E.M.'s *Nightswimming* – a lovely, elegiac song based on just piano, vocals and oboe. The loop is complex and quite long, and well worth a listen.

Taking it further

By now, you should have a reasonable grasp of what it takes to develop skill with lead sheets and comping. As you've probably noticed, the two skills are very closely related. Keep practising on a variety of chord sequences and songs (head to the music shop if you find yourself running out!) and listen to and watch as many pianists as you can.

4: Moving on

In this section we're going to look at some more advanced odds and ends – stuff that's beyond the scope of this book to teach (in some cases it's material you'd struggle to learn from a book, anyway) but which you can begin to explore using the theories and techniques we've looked at so far.

Before we go on, it's worth emphasising that it's a good idea to give yourself a solid grounding in some of the basics we've covered in the book before you get too ambitious. As I've said repeatedly, the trick is to experiment, play around, and let things like chord progressions and common harmonies become instinctive rather than something you have to think hard about every time you play. That's going to take -fair bit of time and a lot of effort – an enjoyable effort, to be sure, but it's worth reiterating that unless you have discovered a hidden genius for piano improvisation, none of the skills we have looked at will come easy. Keep plugging away.

   Second, keep listening to and watching other pianists. As you'll already have gathered, I'm inclined to think that watching is more important than listening. Spend some time exploring YouTube, maybe get hold of a few piano DVDs (suggestions in Appendix 3) and really make a habit of analysing what skilled players do with their hands on the keyboard. If you have fast web access, don't forget look at my own video tutorials, which you can find indexed at:

www.jamcast.co.uk/book

They are completely free and open access, and they go into a lot of detail. If there are parts of the book you have struggled with, the videos should be your first port of call.

More thoughts on improvisation

In Part 2 I described a method that will help you make a start with improvisation: playing around with an increasingly large selection of notes from a relevant scale, over the top of a memorised, possibly patterned, bass part.

That's a great way to make a strong beginning as an improviser, especially if you practise the technique regularly over a long period of time. But although it's a strong beginning, it's certainly not the end of learning about improvisation, and as you gain confidence you'll want to be more adventurous.

Fluent improvisation on any instrument, but especially one as demanding as the piano, has a Zen-like quality to it. It's a bit like riding a bike or cleaning your teeth: once you're good it, it's relatively easy. But the instant you start thinking in detail about all the individual actions involved, it suddenly becomes very difficult. What actually happens when you're improvising – especially at speed – is that your conscious and unconscious minds are working as a team. Your conscious mind guides the overall direction of events, while your unconscious manages the detail, filling in patterns and movements that you've played so many times they are instinctive. This is why repeated, endless, bloody-minded experimentation and practice are essential: if you want to be a good improviser you have to embed chord shapes, scales and riffs so deeply in your unconscious that you can virtually play them with one hand while writing a shopping list or doing a crossword with the other. To a non-improvising musician, improvisation looks like magic. The secret behind that magic lies in the many hours of practice you've spent internalising both the material you've learned from sources like this book, and stuff you've developed for yourself while experimenting at the keyboard.

Beyond that, the route you take depends on the kind of music you're into. If you're interested in jazz, you certainly need to spend some time getting to know a wide variety of jazz chords and scales (you'll find some useful books for this purpose listed in Appendix 3) and familiarising yourself with the jazz 'standards' - the few hundred songs that lie at the heart of the genre.

You'll make quicker progress with your improvisation – whether you've chosen a specific style, or you're dabbling in several – if you play with other musicians. Being part of a band forces discipline upon you, and puts you in a situation where you have to come up with improvisations. It focuses the mind wonderfully. Your best bet, to start with, is to form some sort of informal ensemble with other musicians who have about the same level of ability as you. It's good fun, makes you think hard, and really promotes experimentation.

Some advanced practice ideas

The one essential requirement of being a good musician is lots of practice. But there are good ways to practise, and there are ways that are less good.

First things first: just sitting down and playing the piano is not the same as practising. Consolidation is important, but you need to stretch yourself. Running through material that is easily within your comfort zone can be fun, but it's only marginally effective as a way of improving your ability. Worse, if it involves playing material you don't like, the whole process can be deeply, deadly boring – and if you really want to get better at playing the piano, boredom is your worst enemy. Did you give up the piano when you were a kid? If you did, it's probably because you found all the practice boring.

If you only take notice of two sentences in this section, make it these two:

The secret of effective practice is to make it interesting.
The secret of making practice interesting is to challenge yourself.

Set yourself goals, big and small. These goals might not necessarily be at the top of your mind when you sit down to practise; they might emerge as you play.

- Can I make this scale perfectly even (see p98)?

- Can I add an extra couple of notes to this riff?

- Can I play this piece without a single mistake?

If you take this approach to your piano practice – setting yourself little challenges as you go along, and maybe having one big goal or challenge per session – you'll quickly find it becomes much more absorbing. In fact, it can be addictive: you end up driving yourself and really concentrating hard to meet the challenge you've set. You have to play that line, or riff, or scale just one more time to try to get it perfect. It can be awful for other people to listen to, but as a method of practice it is devastatingly effective: the complete opposite of the boredom that comes from just sitting down at the keyboard and grinding through your scales or set pieces. The basic message is this: branch out. Be experimental.

That's not to say that the 'traditional' way of practising has nothing going for it. It's at least simple and thorough: you run through your scales - in order - before going on to work on the particular piece or pieces you have been assigned for that week. But this approach has its dangers. After a while it's easy to start doing it in a fairly mindless, robotic way – you end up charging through your scales and pieces while your attention wanders. The only benefit you get when this happens is some marginal reinforcement of your recollection of the material you're playing, and a bit of exercise for the muscles in your hands and fingers. It's also a good way of 'sealing in' errors: minor problems of technique that get reinforced every time you make them without either going back to correct yourself or, at the very least, making a mental note to sort them out in the near future.

If you ever get an opportunity to listen to really good musicians practising, you'll notice they constantly push their limits. They often deal with pieces of music in tiny chunks – repeating them over and over, refining them, challenging themselves to play difficult parts perfectly. There's a certain amount of evidence that this habit of working on small segments right at the edge of your ability is one of the most effective practice techniques available, and the one that top performers tend to use to reach very high skill levels. It's sometimes known as *deep practice,* and researchers are doing some fascinating work on the changes it makes in the structure of the brain. The ideas surrounding deep practice put a question mark over our notion of innate musical talent. If you feel yourself to be relatively untalented, you can take heart from the fact that most great musical talents probably weren't born with their abilities, but achieved them through a combination of hard work and deep practice: there's a lot of truth in Thomas Edison's maxim about genius being one percent inspiration and ninety-nine percent perspiration.

There's a good popular overview of deep practice and the associated science in Daniel Coyle's book *The Talent Code* (ISBN-13 978-1847945105), which is well worth a read.

To scale or not to scale?
Scale practice is essential for classical pianists, because it promotes the *legato* style that so much classical playing demands. Pop piano is a bit different, and it's important to stress that extensive scale practice isn't really necessary to learn and develop most of the skills and ideas outlined in this book. But practising your scales - if you can bear it - is worth the effort. Here's why:

• You'll learn and remember the pattern of notes in all the major and minor keys, and when you play music based on those keys (that's nearly all western classical music and the majority of popular music) the notes will fall naturally under your hands.

• I've already stressed the importance of internalisation – fixing skills so deeply in your brain that you don't have to think about them as you play. Scales will help with this. For example, an instinctive knowledge of scales will make it much easier for you to transpose - that is, move a song from one key to another. It will also help you when you try a new song for the first time. Improvisation, too, will become a more instinctive process. In terms of the practical, popular musicianship we're dealing with in this book, those are invaluable skills, and developing them should be reason enough to practise your scales, even if you only do so occasionally.

• One of the main reasons classical pianists must practise their scales so assiduously is that doing so promotes evenness of touch. Playing a run in which each note is equally weighted is very difficult, especially at points where your thumb has to go under your fingers, or you fingers over your thumb. If you practise your scales regularly (and properly - see below) you will find that you develop a much finer degree of control over each individual finger, which ultimately makes for a better, richer, more expressive sound when you play.

You may have noticed that some non-piano instrumentalists often have enough musical knowledge to play the piano in a reasonably sophisticated way - after all, at it's most basic it's just a question of knowing how to map the notes on a score or in your head on to the keys, and, perhaps, of understanding a few basic chord shapes. But that type of player rarely manages a good sound, and is often a bit clunky. Listen to John Lennon playing the piano in *Imagine*, for example. It may be a great song, but he really doesn't sound at home at the keyboard. Non-pianists often get that stilted sound as a result of not having the fine control of touch that a background practising scales brings.

So we've established that practising your scales is useful, if not essential, for what we're trying to do. But what if you've only done a couple of grades on piano, and only know some very basic scales? And what about the issue we mentioned above, of practising them properly? Well, to start with, learning new scales is easy: there are plenty of scale books available – the most useful is ABRSM's *Manual of Scales, Broken Chords and Arpeggios for Piano*, which I've included in the book list in Appendix 3.

But how do you make sure you're doing it right?

Here are some tips:

• Watch out for the autopilot trap. Once you get good at playing scales, it's easy just to whizz through them without paying attention to what your fingers are doing. Concentrate!

• Aim for the evenness of touch I mentioned above. A good trick here is to record yourself playing: you are aiming for a result where all the notes sound perfectly even, with not even the slightest extra pressure or emphasis when your fingers cross (which is the point at which you're most likely to get an uneven sound). Achieving a very high level of evenness takes a lot of hard work and isn't something you really need to aim for unless you're intending to become a good classical pianist. However, as a way of improving your fine finger control (useful for all types of piano playing) it just can't be beaten.

• Try breaking your scales up into small chunks. For example, try running down a scale of F major in your right hand, but just from E to B♭. You'll be fingering 3-2-1 (to the C) and then putting your fourth finger over on to the B♭. Practise swinging that fourth finger over the instant your thumb hits the C.

• Again, unless you're aiming for a very high level of classical achievement, you needn't practise your scales everyday. However, the more you do, the more comfortable you'll be on the keyboard – providing you're practising them correctly.

Key variety

As I've said, one of the great things about scales is that they help you settle comfortably into different keys. On that subject, it's worth saying that you should get used to playing and improvising in a variety of keys as soon as possible. You'll make much better progress if you branch out from playing solely in the keys I've used in the examples. If you don't, somewhere along the line you'll find yourself 'trapped' and only able to play well in a limited range. That's not such a big deal if you're only playing for your own pleasure, but it will be a problem if you're going to be playing in bands or with a singer.

Playing by ear

Playing by ear – the process of working out how to play a song having only listened to it – is difficult. Some people, generally those with a very good sense of the relative pitch of different notes and chords, can do it very well. Others have to work at it. Most pianists can learn to play by ear to at least a reasonable level of competence.

There are two basic types of ear playing: the first is the ability gradually to work out how a song should be played, having heard it a few times. The second is the ability to do so on the spot, perhaps only having heard the song once or twice. The natural quality of your ear (which might be better than you think, once you start working on it) will go a long way to determining whether you can master the second type, as will your willingness to work on the skill.

Unless you're the sort of natural who can instantly pick out tunes on the piano having heard them only once, you're going to need to do a fair bit of work to master ear playing. However, as you practise and experiment at the piano, you'll find that you internalise many of the skills required.

Melody

When a melody moves from one note to another it is doing one of two things: either moving up or down a scale (usually the scale of the key you're playing the song in) or making an interval jump. Spotting scalar movement is fairly easy. However, the key to playing a melody from ear is having a good grasp of intervals. Experience of choral singing will make a big difference here, but you can also practise your interval spotting using the tools at www.musictheory.net.

Chord progression

It's slightly harder to identify harmonic structures than it is to pick out a tune, but not by much. This is because the harmony of most popular songs is quite regular, and familiar patterns soon emerge. Some chord progressions are very common indeed (remember the progression in *E Flat Lead Sheet* in Part 3?). If you play lots of different songs you'll find you get a sense of how different chord progressions sound. If you've worked out the melody of the song you're trying to play, it'll also give you some clues about how the harmony is going to work.

Once you've figured out melody and chord progression, you've essentially got the same information you'd get from a lead sheet, and can use the techniques we looked at in Part 3 to work on it from there. If you want to become a good ear player, the trick – as with so much else – is to practise regularly. We all hear new music every day, whether it's a mobile ringtone or part of a TV ad. When a tune lodges in your head, sit down at the piano and try to work it out. This is a good practice technique for more than just ear playing – it'll help you further refine your sense of how melody and harmony work together at a deep level, which is an important part of all the skills we've looked at.

Ear comping

It's worth noting, briefly, that working out a comp by ear is, actually, easier than figuring out how to play the equivalent full song as a solo – because all you have to do is identify the chord sequence and play along, with no melody required. If you have to comp by ear, it'll usually be as part of a band, which should also help to cover your mistakes, if you make any. A really good practice technique is to work with tracks from your music collection. If you have an iPod or similar MP3 player, use it to listen to tunes while you try playing along. Choose one or two songs, see if you can work out the chord progression, and try 'joining in', perhaps just playing the chords in blocks at first. Again, this is a practice technique that has value far beyond ear playing.

Final word

I hope all of this has been of some use to you. If you have any questions or comments, there are two ways of getting in touch with me. First, there are quite a few posts about piano playing on my blog at www.jamcast.co.uk. Feel free to add comments: other people will benefit from reading about shared difficulties, and I'll always reply.

I'll also reply if you email me – bill@billhilton.biz. I welcome anything you have to say, including suggestions for future editions of the book.

Happy piano playing!

Bill Hilton was born in Boston, Lincolnshire in 1974 and educated at Boston Grammar School and the University of Wales, Bangor. He started playing the piano at eight, and has performed solo and in bands at hundreds of live gigs.

When he's not playing the piano, Bill is a freelance copywriter and journalist, and has one previous book to his name - *Working for Yourself, A Which? Essential Guide* (with Mike Pywell). He also runs the musicianship blog Jamcast (www.jamcast.co.uk).

Bill lives in North Wales.

Appendix 1: Theory Resources and Intervals

Music theory is a whole subject in itself, and covering everything you need to know is way beyond the scope of this book. I have, however, included a short section explaining intervals and their terminology, simply because they are important to many of the concepts discussed in the previous pages. As a piano student, you typically won't find out much about intervals until you are several years into lessons. You'll find this is especially true if you've had classical lessons in the past few years, as the requirement to identify and sing intervals is no longer as prominent as it once was in examinations.

If, in the course of using this book, you've come across other areas of theory you have found unfamiliar, there are quite a few resources you can turn to for help.

Books

There are hundreds of books on theory, many of them academic tomes that tell you far more than you'll ever need to know to handle the material here. One of the most comprehensive is *The AB Guide to Music Theory, Part 1* by Eric Taylor (ISBN-13: 978-1854724465). Taylor's *Guide* covers all the subjects in the Associated Board theory examinations from Grade 1 to Grade 5. It's very clear and comprehensive. If you get really into your theory you could also buy Part 2, which covers Grades 6 to 8.

Music Theory for Dummies by Holly Day and Michael Pilhofer (ISBN-13: 978-0764578380) covers everything you need to know in a very relaxed and accessible style. It includes sections on intervals and chords, which might be useful if you want a different perspective from the one offered here. If you search Google Books (http://books.google.com) you'll find almost the whole thing, for free. A few dozen pages are missed out to encourage you to buy the print edition, but you can get an idea of the contents before committing your cash. One small problem is that the authors don't provide British 'translations' of American terms. So you have to remember that a 'quarter note' is a crotchet, a 'half note' is a minim, a 'measure' is a bar and so on.

The web

I've already mentioned Google Books, which features several good music theory titles, although *Music Theory for Dummies* is one of the few available in its entirety.

As you might imagine, Wikipedia has a comprehensive selection of articles on music theory (start here: http://en.wikipedia.org/wiki/Music_theory). Many of them include audio samples, which are useful if you're trying to understand what particular intervals and scales sound like. On the other hand, some of the articles go into a serious level of detail, so you need to be either a very good skim reader or very interested in theory if you're going to find them useful as a quick look-up.

In the next chapter, you'll find charts of many popular chords and scales. However, if you're looking for very complex chords, the Piano World Chord Tool is absolutely outstanding: www.pianoworld.com/fun/vpc/piano_chords.htm - select the chord or scale from the drop-down box, and it displays it right there on a virtual keyboard.

Ricci Adam's www.musictheory.net also includes a chord tool, along with a range of other very helpful features. There's an interactive guide to music theory and a 'training' section where you can test your knowledge of chords and intervals, which turns out to be surprisingly addictive...

An overview of intervals

Several of the resources above contain very comprehensive guides to intervals, but because intervals are so important to the ideas discussed in this book, I thought it would be handy to include a brief explanation here, too.

An interval is the distance between two notes. You might sometimes read about *harmonic* and *melodic* intervals: the former is when two notes are played together (i.e., in harmony) and the latter when they are played one after the other (i.e., as part of a melody). The difference isn't that important. Here are some harmonic intervals:

perfect 4th   major 3rd   minor 3rd   major 6th   minor 6th

And here are the same intervals, in melodic form:

perfect 4th   major 3rd   minor 3rd   major 6th   minor 6th

Intervals have both *quantity* and *quality*. An interval's quantity is the raw distance between the two notes. The basic quantities are unison, second, third, fourth, fifth, sixth, seventh and octave. The easiest way to determine an interval's quantity when it is written down is to count the number of stave lines and spaces between the two notes, including the lines or spaces that the notes are actually on. So, for example, we can see that this interval is spread over six lines and spaces, meaning it is some sort of sixth:

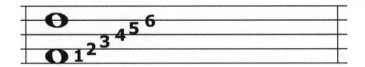

While this one takes up three lines and spaces, so it is some sort of third:

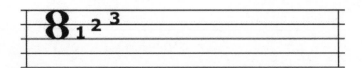

If you look at an eight-note scale, major or minor, you'll see that each subsequent note of the scale is a degree of quantity further away from the tonic. Play two identical notes together (which you can't on one piano, obviously) and your 'interval' is unison. Play the root with the next note of the scale, and the interval is a second, with the next, and it's a third.

(unison)   second   third   fourth   fifth   sixth   seventh   octave

An interval doesn't have to include the tonic note of a scale. If it doesn't, you can work out its quantity by subtracting the lower note's distance from the tonic from the higher note's distance from the tonic, and adding one. So, for example, the interval between the third and the seventh note of a scale is 7 - 3 + 1 = 5, a fifth. If you're looking at intervals in notated form things are even easier, because, as we've seen, all you have to do is count the number of lines and spaces the interval occupies.

It's quite possible to have intervals greater than an octave. These are *compound intervals*, and the one that's mentioned most in this book is the ninth. A ninth is the same note as a second (e.g., a D in C major). However, when you're building chords it's useful to think of the note as the ninth degree of the scale - a major or minor third above the note which is used to create the various types of seventh chord, upon which ninth chords are based. This shows B as the ninth interval above A:

Quality

An interval's quality can be major, minor, perfect, augmented or diminished. Minor intervals have an upper note that is a semitone lower than their major equivalents. For example, both of these intervals are sevenths, but the first is a major seventh while the second is minor:

Major and minor third:

Major and minor second:

Intervals of a second (major or minor) are sometimes just referred to as a whole tone (major second) or a semitone (minor second) - there's a full explantion in the footnote on p15. There are two minor second intervals in a major scale: between the third and fourth notes (E and F in C major) and the seventh and eighth (B and C in C major).

Only seconds, thirds, sixths and sevenths can be major or minor. The intervals of a fourth and a fifth are usually referred to as 'perfect fourth' and 'perfect fifth'. That is because they are always the same in both major and minor scales.

For example, if we're in the key of C major and we play the note a third above the tonic, the interval is a major third:

major 3rd

In C minor, if we play the note a third above the tonic, the interval is a minor third:

minor 3rd

Whereas the fourth and fifth notes are the same in both keys:

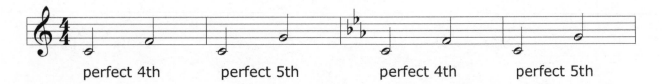

perfect 4th   perfect 5th   perfect 4th   perfect 5th

In augmented and diminished intervals the upper note is sharpened (augmented) or flattened (diminished) by a semitone, irrespective of key:

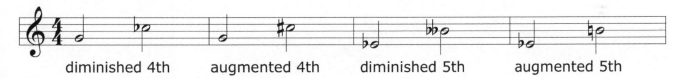

diminished 4th   augmented 4th   diminished 5th   augmented 5th

They are still fifths - count the lines and spaces they occupy on the stave. You may have noticed that some intervals can have two names: an augmented fifth is identical (in terms of the distance between notes) to a minor sixth. However, this difference depends on context, and is pretty academic.

And that, really, is it. If you feel you need any extra information on intervals, the resources listed on pp105-106 are excellent. In particular, take a look at the interactive tutorials on intervals at www.musicroom.net, which are very useful. I've also created a video tutorial about interval basics. You'll find it listed in the index of tutorials at:

www.jamcast.co.uk/book

Appendix 2: Blues Scales and Chord Tables

Blues Scales

Overleaf are blues scales for each note of the twelve-tone scale. I've included these to help you practise the blues improvisation techniques described in Part 2. Unlike the chord charts (which start on p114), I haven't duplicated scales for both names of each black note, on the basis that if a blues is in a black-note key it's almost always referred to in the flat key belonging to that note. In other words, while you won't come across many blues-type pieces notated in A#, there are an awful lot in B♭.

In case you're not sure, a double flat (♭♭) takes a note down *two* semitones rather than one, so A double-flat (A♭♭) is the same note on the keyboard as G.

Note: Including a comprehensive list of standard major and minor scales is beyond the scope of this book. If your piano lessons were a long time ago, and consequently you're struggling with scales, check out the ABRSM *Manual of Scales* - full details of which can be found in Appendix 3.

Key   **Blues Scale**

Key   **Blues Scale**

Table of Chords

A few notes to aid your understanding of the look-up tables, which start opposite:

1. Each of these tables features the most common chords for any given tonic note. More unusual chords have been omitted. If, in your daily playing, you come across a chord you don't know, look it up online or use one of the guides listed in Appendix 3.

2. All chords are written in the treble clef. I've not included bass voicings (Dm7/G, F/G etc.) on the basis that these are easy to work out for yourself; see p42 for details.

3. Most of the chords (except those indicated in point 6, below) are notated in all basic inversions, starting with root position. See pp20-21 for an explanation of inversions.

4. Chords are organised based on their tonic note (all C chords, all G# chords and so on). Because this section is intended as a quick look-up resource, each black note has two tables – one for its sharp name and one for its flat name. So the chords in the C# table use exactly the same notes as the one in the D♭ table, but are differently notated. I've not included tables for E#, F♭, B# and C♭, because they are virtually never used in popular music.

5. I've notated the diminished chords using *dim*. Strictly speaking, *dim* indicates a three-note diminished triad, while the four-note diminished seventh should be notated as *dim7*. However, with the exception of some contemporary jazz lead sheets, if you see *dim* in chords for popular music it almost always indicates a diminished seventh.

6. Strictly speaking, ninth chords, both major and minor, have a root position and four inversions, but some of these are very unusual. For 9s I've missed out the root (which is rare) and included four common voicings – these would usually be played with an appropriate root in the bass to give the chord its proper context. I've included maj9s for completeness, and only in their root positions – they tend to invert in all kinds of weird ways that aren't worth going into in a general guide.

7. Remember a double flat (♭♭) takes a note down two semitones rather than one. A double sharp (✕) takes it up two semitones instead of one. So G double-sharp (G✕) is the same note as A, and A double-flat (A♭♭) is the same as G. There are several double accidentals in these tables, but they shouldn't cause you too many problems. As a rule, the scarier a chord looks, the less often you'll find it in a progression.

C

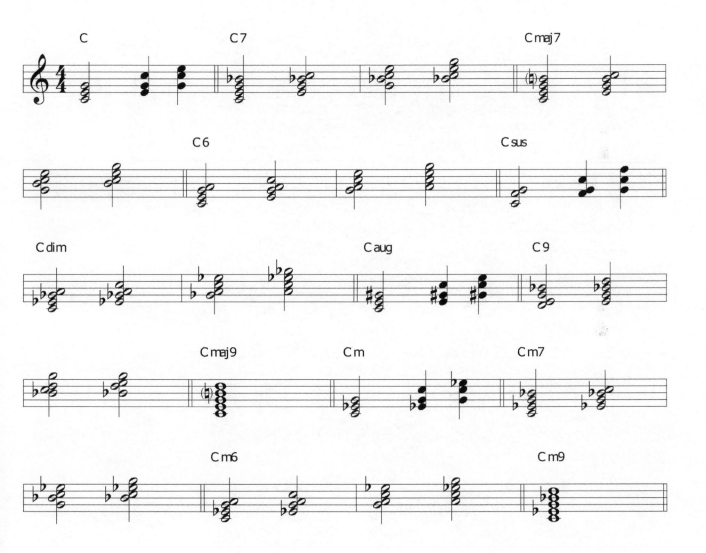

C#

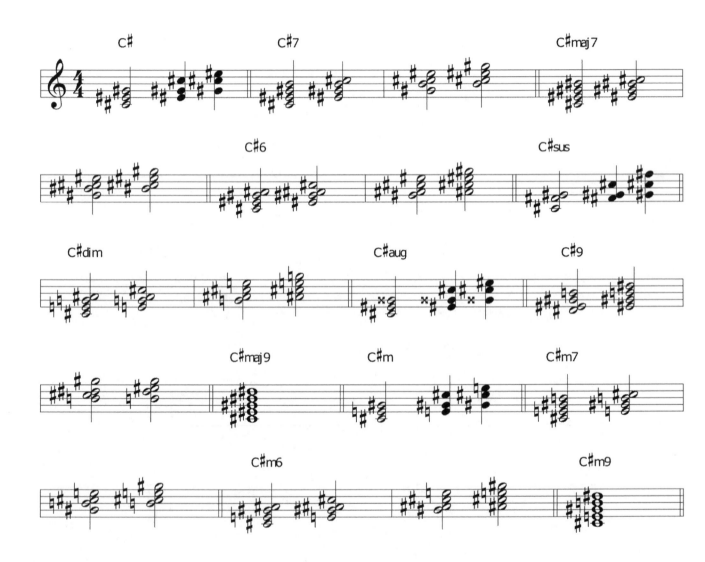

D♭

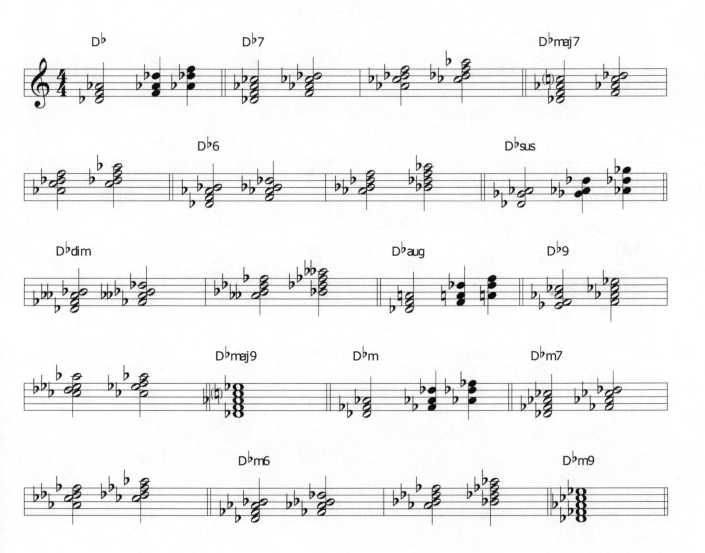

D

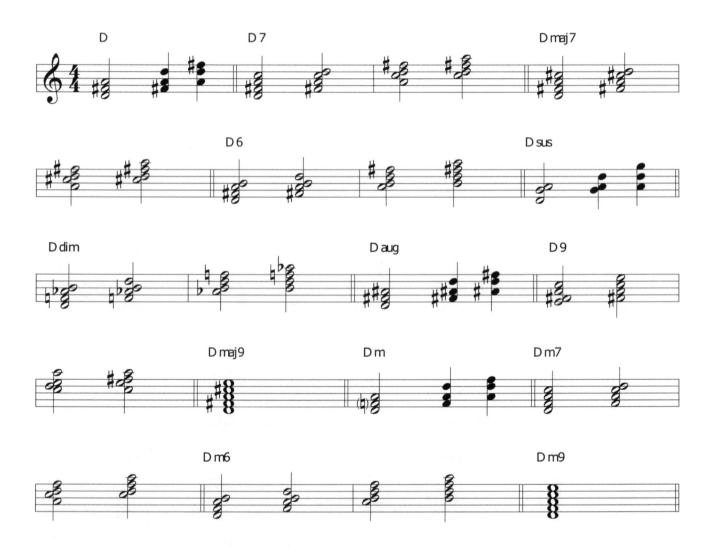

D#

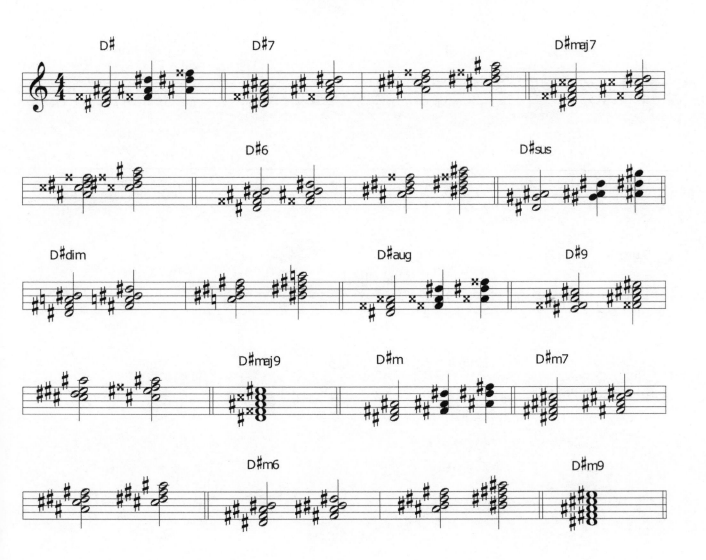

E♭

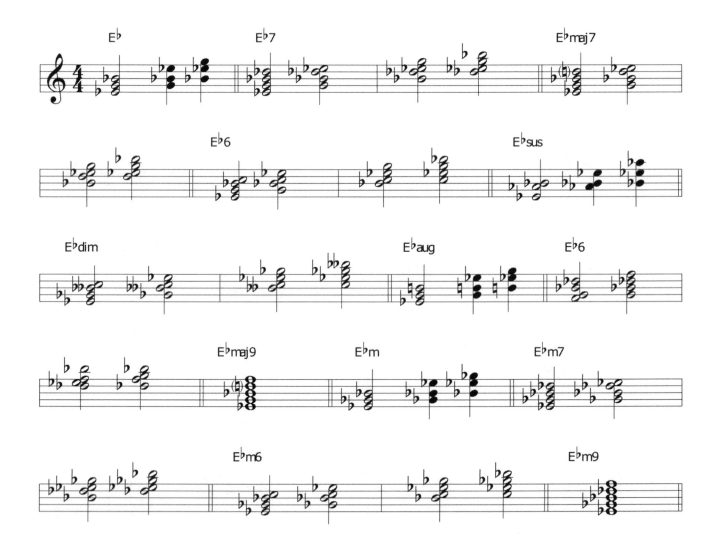

E

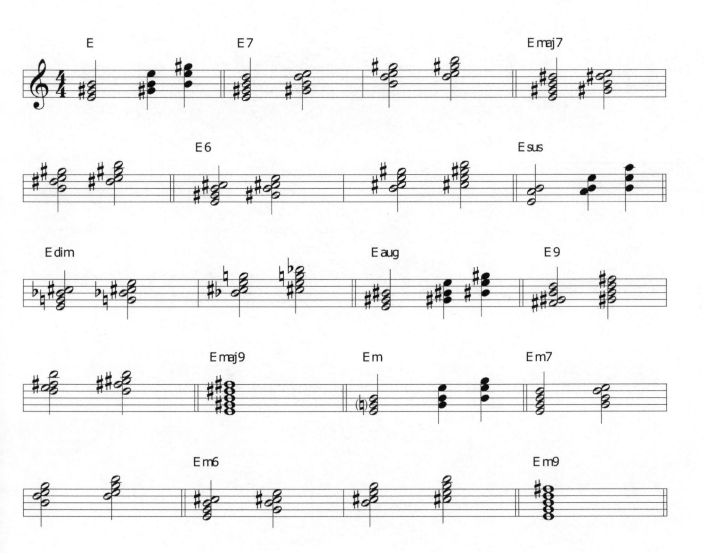

F

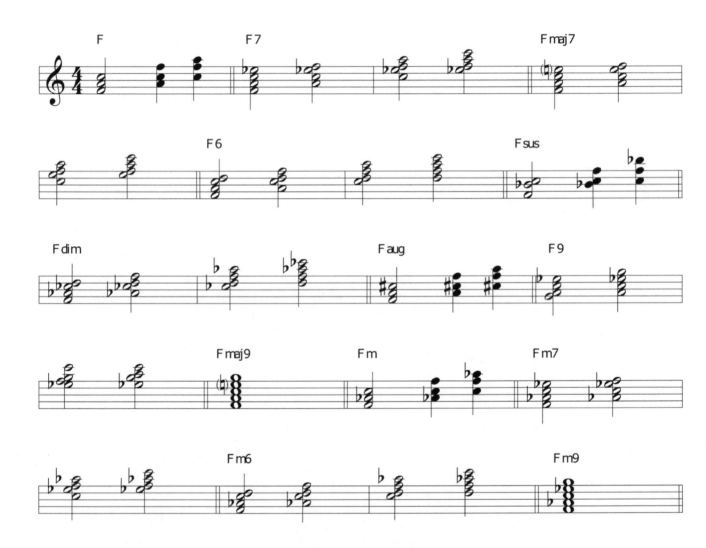

F#

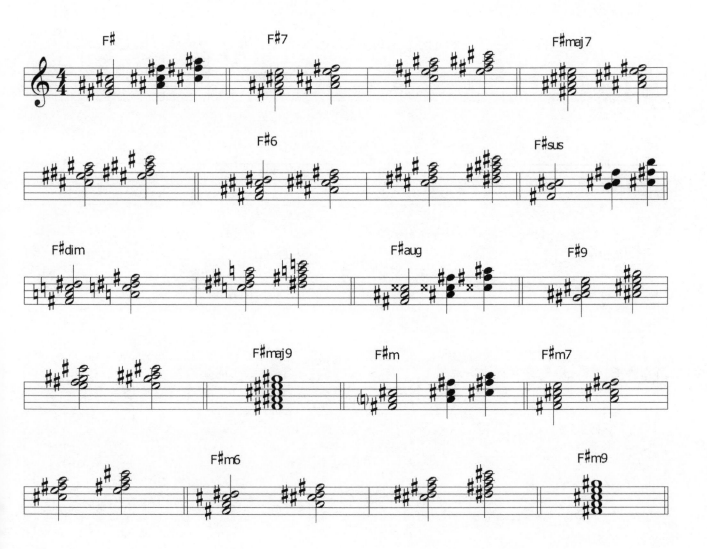

G♭

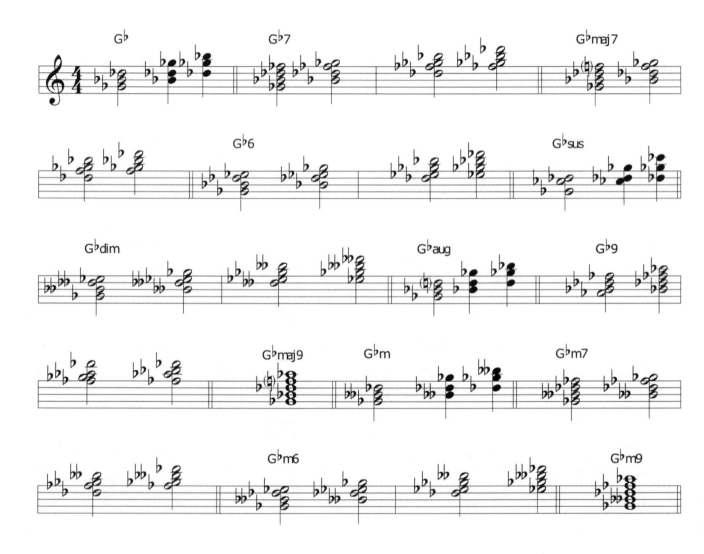

G

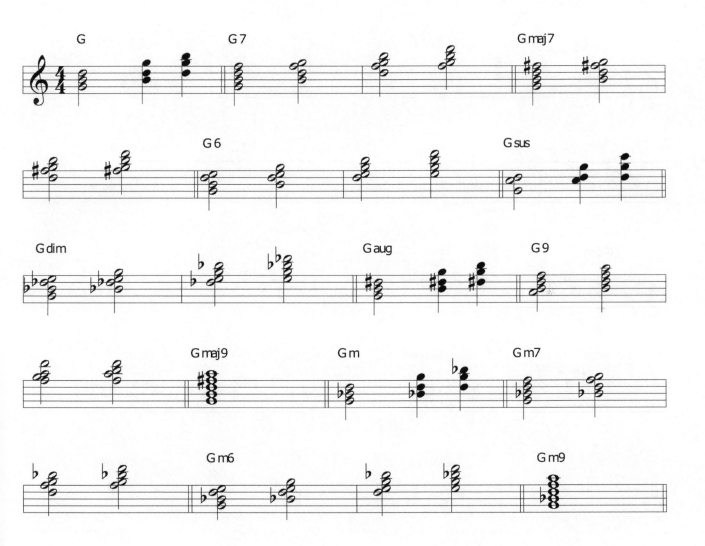

G#

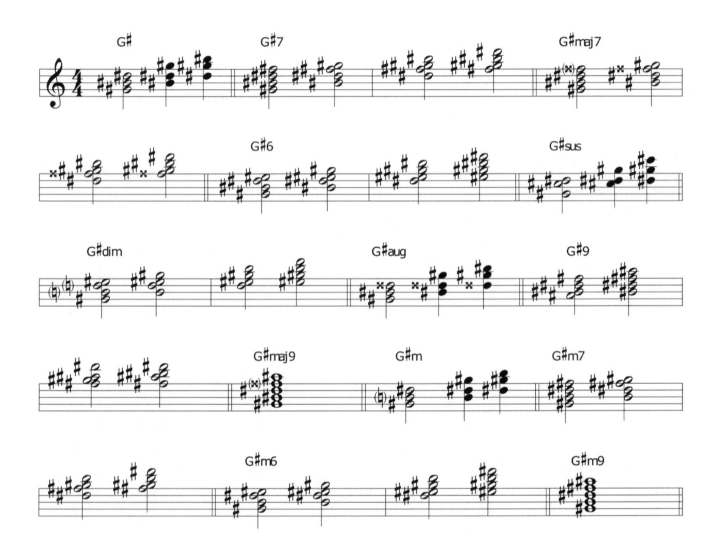

A♭

A#

B♭

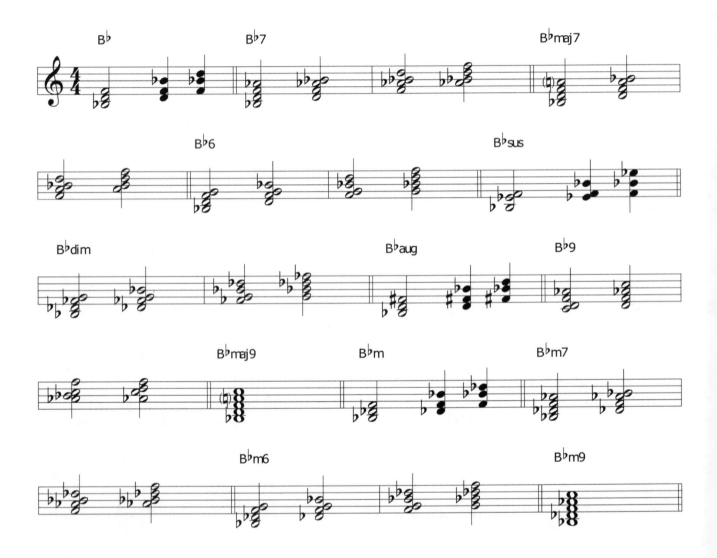

B

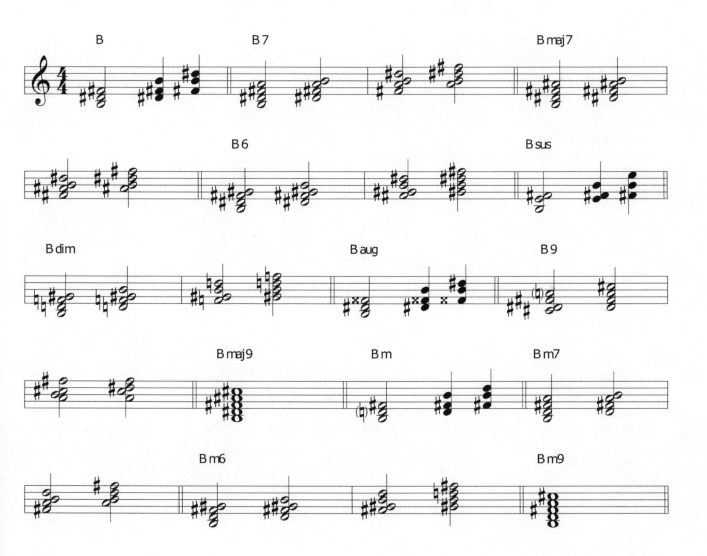

Appendix 3: Useful Books and DVDs

DVDs

Martin Scorsese Presents The Blues: Piano Blues

[DVD – CD also available: 2004]

This is part of a series of films produced by renowned director Scorcese, who is passionate about blues music. His fellow enthusiast Clint Eastwood presents this episode. There's lots of great close-up action of seriously skilled pianists at work, plus interviews with greats such as Ray Charles, Dr John and Marcia Ball.

The Piano Styles of Dr John

[DVD: 2003]

A selection of performances from living legend Dr John (Mac Rebennack), one of the world's greatest practitioners of blues and New Orleans jazz on the piano. There are quite a few Dr John DVDs available. I recommend this one chiefly because it's got so much good content and it includes booklets of sheet music so you can analyse the songs in detail. By the way, Dr John also has a tutorial DVD called *Dr John Teaches New Orleans Piano*. I haven't seen it yet, but it's got to be worth a look if blues and boogie-woogie is your thing.

Elton John – Red Piano

[2 DVDs + CD: 2008]

Elton John is a first-rate pianist, and somebody you have to watch if you want to comp along with contemporary pop, rock or folk. There's a lot of movement in his style, and a very broad dynamic range. There are plenty of Elton John DVDs on the market. This one is from the Red Piano tour, and features many of his classic songs.

Ben Folds – Live at MySpace

[DVD: 2007]

This is a short DVD of a gig that Ben Folds did as a webcast on MySpace.com, live from his own studio in Nashville. It's interesting because it all takes place in front of quite a small audience and you can really get a detailed sense of what Folds is doing on the piano (and the various other instruments he plays). My personal favourite on the DVD is his cover of *Such Great Heights*, originally by the band The Postal Service. He stuffs his grand piano full of shirts to get a dampened effect and plays a quick groove to mimic the quick dance beat of the original.

(At the time of writing, most of the DVD is available as fairly low-quality clips on YouTube.com. They aren't official though, so they might not still be there by the time you read this. Look for 'Ben Folds Myspace' using the site's search function. By the way, you need to be aware that the DVD and clips contain lots of fruity language, so don't go buying this for your granny unless she's on the broadminded side.)

Oscar Peterson – The Berlin Concert

[DVD: 2007]

Peterson was arguably past his peak by the time he gave this concert, but it's one of the best piano DVDs available. Pure pianistic awesomeness.

Ray Charles - The Legend Live

[DVD: 2006]

Charles is interesting because he's a great pianist who straddles two eras: he plays New Orleans blues like Dr John, dabbles in jazz and comes up to date with R'n'B and soul sounds. While he's not a technical genius in the way Peterson is, Charles plays the piano with a lot of character and skill.

Books

I've already mentioned one or two titles in the main sections of the book. Here's a short list of a few more that you might find useful.

The Keyboardist's Picture Chord Encyclopedia
by Leonard Vogler (ISBN-13: 978-0825611322)
There are quite a few chord encyclopedias on the market, and this is one of the most useful and comprehensive. As well as the notation for each chord, Vogler includes a photo of how it's played on the keyboard: useful if you're not a hugely confident reader of music, or you get fed up translating endless sharps and flats into real notes.

The Manual Of Scales, Broken Chords and Arpeggios For Piano
ed. Ruth Gerald (ISBN-13: 978-1860961120)
If you want to be a better all-round pianist, getting in some scale practice is essential. But if it's a long time since you played your scales, they might be a bit rusty. This book – which is designed for students taking Associated Board exams – is a comprehensive resource, and includes every standard scale (but not the jazz ones) you'll ever need, plus the necessary fingerings.

Jazz Exercises, Minuets, Etudes and Pieces for Piano
by Oscar Peterson (ISBN-13: 978-0634099793)
This is a really useful book if you're interested in developing your jazz and blues skills further (although Peterson is usually referred to as a 'jazz pianist', he played in both genres). It'll also come in useful if you're interested in playing any kind of pop from the jazz age. Aimed primarily at pianists with a basic classical training, Peterson's book offers a series of exercises designed to get you thinking like an improviser. He includes some useful material on blues, boogie-woogie and walking basses. His introduction – which sets out how 'jazz' piano is different from 'classical' piano – is also invaluable.

Jazz Piano Scales: Grades 1-5

ABRSM (ISBN-13: 978-1860960086)

If you really want to dedicate yourself to jazz, some knowledge of the different jazz scales (of which the blues scale is the oldest and most well-known) is essential. This book is based around the Associated Board Jazz syllabus. I have a few reservations about applying the grade system to jazz playing – jazz piano is supposed to be about having a good time, not competing for certificates – but there's no doubt that this book is really useful for would-be jazzers.

The Ultimate Fake Book: C Edition

Hal Leonard Corporation (ISBN-13: 978-0793529391)

There are lots of fake books on the market (see p70 for an explanation of what they are), but this is probably the most comprehensive general one available. With over a thousand lead sheets in a variety of genres, it'll keep you going for some time, and prove invaluable if you ever take up gigging at weddings and parties. I particularly like it because it is comb-bound, so it lays flat easily. The downside of this is that you have to be careful how you handle it, as combs aren't as robust as good-quality perfect binds. Treat it well, and it should last for years.

Lightning Source UK Ltd.
Milton Keynes UK
21 February 2011

167908UK00006B/5/P